Political Economy of Malaysia's Industrial Policy

Firdausi Suffian

Political Economy of Malaysia's Industrial Policy

Institutional Capacity and the Automotive Industry

Springer

Firdausi Suffian
Faculty of Administrative Science and Policy Studies
Universiti Teknologi MARA
Kota Kinabalu, Sabah, Malaysia

ISBN 978-981-33-6900-9 ISBN 978-981-33-6901-6 (eBook)
https://doi.org/10.1007/978-981-33-6901-6

This Springer imprint is published by the registered company Springer Nature Singapore Pte Ltd.
The registered company address is: 152 Beach Road, #21-01/04 Gateway East, Singapore 189721, Singapore

To my family.

Foreword

In the annals of industrialisation, Malaysia has achieved a double first. It was the first Muslim-majority country to industrialise and most unusually for a capitalist economy, it has done so with a redistribution policy at the heart of its development project. Given that it is also one of the only two multiracial industrialised countries in East Asia (the other is Singapore), Malaysia could well stand as a beacon of hope to other countries of the Global South that have yet to industrialise. Unfortunately, Malaysia's ability to be seen as a development guide now seems less credible than it was 20 years ago. Dr. Suffian's excellent interrogation of the political economy of Malaysia's automobile industry helps us understand the challenges industrialising the country and institutional constraints

With independence in 1957, what later became the new country of Malaysia was bequeathed four important legacies by its British colonisers: an economy composed of plantation and peasant agriculture, tin mining and trade-based commerce; a racial division of labour (Malay/Bumiputra, Chinese, Indian) that reflected the economic structure; poverty and inequality that partly reflected the division of labour; and a bifurcation of power whereby Chinese Malaysians largely controlled the economy and Malays/Bumiputra, the state. Perhaps inevitably, the contradictions inherent in these arrangements led to interracial conflict in the late 1960s. For the Malaysian government, the way forward was industrialisation (thus increasing employment and reducing poverty) and this was achieved largely by means of foreign investment in the assembly of electronics products.

By the 1980s a concern to emulate the Northeast Asian economies led to a heavy industrialisation programme of which the centrepiece was an automobile industry. Driven by economic nationalism, the first auto firm—Proton—was initially a joint venture between the state's Heavy Industries Commission and Mitsubishi. Complemented by the Perodua brand in the 1990s and protected from foreign imports by very high tariffs (up to 300% until the mid-2000s) on the domestic market, the 'national car' project—in terms of production scale, innovation, skill upgrading and export market penetration has been—at best—a limited success. In terms of the state's redistribution agenda, however, it has been more successful. Whereas the opportunities for local firm linkages created by the electronics subsidiaries were seized by Chinese

Malaysian entrepreneurs, thanks to state patronage, those spawned by the national car project were made available to Bumiputra ones.

In *The Political Economy of Malaysia's Industrial Policy: Institutional Capacity and the Automotive Industry*, Firdausi Suffian meticulously charts the political–economic dynamics and considerations that forged and continue to influence the development of Malaysia's auto industry. In so doing he shows how the articulation of elite interests with the state's redistributional agenda has helped deliver the industry—for better or worse—to its current condition. While other books have analysed this scene at a macro level, this is the only one to have 'drilled down' into the interstices of an industry essential to Malaysia's socio-economic development project. In this very important contribution, Dr. Suffian exposes some of the detail of why Malaysia may have 'stalled' as an industrial economy and why it may be already in the early stages of deindustrialisation.

Jeffrey Henderson
Professor Emeritus of International Development
University of Bristol, Bristol, UK

Acknowledgements

This book is based on my Ph.D. research in University of Bristol on Malaysia industrial policy between 2014 and 2017. I would like to thank my supervisor Emeritus Professor Jeffery Henderson and Dr. Gaston Fornes for guiding me to complete this research. I am very pleased with both of my supervisor who introduced theory of institutionalism to assess industrial policy in Malaysia. Such theory provides new ways of thinking in analysing political economy of industrial policy, particularly in automotive industry. Application of the theory provides valuable insights on the political and economic dynamics in industrial policy formulations and implementation. I would also like to thank Emeritus Professor John Thoburn who has also helped me further understand Malaysia's industrial policy and automotive industry.

I would like to express my gratitude to all the top officials in the government ministries, heads of corporate and business associations, leading academicians, local research institutes and senior politicians who agreed to become interviewees during the data collection processes. Special thanks to former Prime Minister Dr. Mahathir Mohammad who is also the brainchild of the national car project for providing valuable information during the interview.

My gratitude also goes to Kamal Solhaimi Fadzil, Tan Sri Kamal Salih for helping me during my data collection process and framing my case study. This includes Prof. Rajah Rasiah and Prof. Terence Gomez who have provided valuable insights on Malaysia's political economy.

Contents

Abstract

This book explores the political economy of industrial policy-making process in Malaysia, specifically in the national automotive policy (NAP). The automotive sector is one of the sectional interests under the heavy industrialisation programme introduced by the government during Dr. Mahathir Mohammad as Prime Minister (1981–2003). Often in Malaysia's policy-making process, the government manages the need for modernising the country through industrial development. It also responds to the domestic political economy including political pressure, domestic enterprise interest and ethno-economic development. This highlights the need to understand the dynamics of the political economy of industrial policy-making process. To uncover the political and economic aspects of the national automotive policy, this study seeks to explore what institutional arrangements evolve around the national automotive policy and how the state elite (politicians and bureaucrats) and 'selected' business groups mobilise, coordinate and prioritise resources and economic preferences in the policy-making institutions.

The findings show that the political elites have a paternalistic role in policy decisions. As a consequence, the political elites can assert policy preferences along with the interest of the Bumiputra industrialist class. Formation of the NAP was part of an effort to liberalise the domestic automotive sector to create a level playing field environment, various institutional arrangements are in fact made to protect the domestic enterprises' interests. The terms of policy have limited pro-market reforms. The reciprocal relationship between policy actors and 'selected' business enterprises enable them to configure and interpret policy in a way that favours their interests. Domestic automotive enterprises have benefitted from various state resources beyond arm's length relationships. Furthermore, the ethno-economic consideration (i.e. Bumiputra interest) is 'packaged' in the policy as part of protecting the domestic automotive sectors. This study shows how political influences in the automotive sector are crucial to facilitate the growth of Proton, the country's flagship national car manufacturer, though they have a constraining effect on the direction of the national carmaker. Political consideration and ethno-nationalist interest have generally limited the growth of Proton.

Overall, this study shows that existing institutional structures influenced by historical events, political factors, power relations and norms have enabled a 'triangular arrangement' between state elites (politicians and bureaucrats) and 'selected' enterprises to formulate policy. Institutional arrangements made by these actors reveal the complex relationships and interactions among elite policy actors to influence the policy-making process. Often, political consideration precedes economic rationale. This has implications on policy-making institutions, which in turn affects their developmental strategy.

Chapter 1
Introduction

1.1 Malaysian Industrial Development

Malaysia, one of the largest economies in Southeast Asia, has attained significant economic development. Industrialisation has become one of the central considerations in modernising the country's economy, which has effectively transformed from primarily commodity-dominated activities to an industrial-based economy. Industrial policy is devised for industrialising the country and has undergone several phases over the past decades. During the post-colonial period (1958–1969) industrial policy favoured Import Substituting Industrialisation (ISI) in seeking to expand the domestic industrial base and encourage learning-by-doing (Jomo, 1993). This was part of economic diversification efforts to reduce over-reliance on commodity activities like rubber and tin (Tan, 2014). The industrial policy at this stage was to provide tax exemptions, infrastructures and imposition of tariff protections. Though ISI increased manufacturing activities (mainly dominated by Chinese-owned firms), it was limited by the small domestic market (Rasiah, 2011a). The policy failed to move beyond basic manufacturing assembly activities, and little productions went into the export market (Jomo & Edward, 1993). Import of capital and intermediate goods rose rapidly between the year 1963—1968 consequently aggravated balance of trade. ISI, unable to absorb excess of labour, led to high unemployment. The economy faced income disparities and high poverty incidence across ethnic groups (Lall, 1995).

The industrial policy shifted to Export Oriented Industrialisation (EOI) from 1970 to 1980, facilitated by the global production network relocating activities to developing countries (especially the semiconductor industry). The Investment Incentive Act 1968 was enacted and established the Free Trade Zone (FTZ). The EOI strategy was to promote FDI-led export manufacturing activities and to create linkages and upgrading. Export activities mainly attract FDI labour-intensive industries and firms were given lucrative tax exemptions. Restricted labour rights were also part of the policy to attract FDI (Jomo, 1993). Vast relocation of foreign companies has

F. Suffian, *Political Economy of Malaysia's Industrial Policy*,
https://doi.org/10.1007/978-981-33-6901-6_1

facilitated export activities, reduce unemployment rates, transfer of low-mid technology and building linkages with domestic industry. Malaysia's manufacturing grew rapidly, particularly in the electronics and electrical sectors, as well as in the textile and clothing industry (Rasiah, 2011a). However, the EOI strategy constrained the growth of industrial development. The manufacturing activities did not move up the value chain due to lack of effective linkages with foreign companies. This resulted in industrial dualism, where a foreign company controls high technological activities while the domestic firms are restricted to assembly and subcontracting (Tan, 2014). Recognising this problem, the government prompted a shift from low-mid tier activities characterised by labour intensity to more capital-intensive activity (Menon, 2008).

In 1970 the government introduced the New Economic Policy (NEP) in wake of the racial tensions in 1969. The racial riot occurred due to economic inequality was expressed in a communal sense. The Bumiputra's main economic activities were mainly in agricultural activities, while the Chinese focused on commercial activities. The post-colonial government which emphasised the ISI strategy that somehow favours Chinese entrepreneurs made feeble attempts to increase participation of Bumiputra in economic activity. This has led to a serious gap between these two major ethnic groups. To reduce inequality, NEP had a two-pronged goal of alleviating poverty and restructuring society. The effort to 'restructure society' sought to reduce inter-ethnic economic disparities especially for Bumiputra,[1] by eliminating the identification of race with economic functions (Jomo & Wee, 2014). The NEP gave the state direct intervention in economic development. Industrial development has since been tailored along the need in the NEP to redress socio-economic inequality (Rasiah & Shari, 2001). Various state-owned enterprises were formed to facilitate the growth of Bumiputra entrepreneurs. The government also fosters the growth of Bumiputra suppliers in manufacturing activities. Bumiputra business groups are given strong preferences and special privileges in terms of financing, education, skills and training, and licenses, among others.

In the 1980's the government launched the second round of ISI strategy under the Fourth Malaysia Plan (1981–1985). This industrial policy earmarked a heavy industrialisation programme in which technological acquisition, industrial upgrading, and research and development (R&D) activity became a central part of industrial policy. The purpose of the heavy industrialisation was to develop indigenous technology capabilities. The heavy industrialisation programme emulates South Korea and Japan in strengthening their industrial base. The Heavy Industries Corporation of Malaysia (HICOM) was established to diversify manufacturing activities and develop forward and backward linkages. The programme saw the growth of steel, cement, and more importantly, transport equipment and automotive sectors. Heavy industry enjoyed strong protections (tariff and non-tariff barriers) and subsidies. The government-sponsored heavy industry projects have had limited success due to long gestation

[1] Bumiputra refers to the indigenous people in Malaysia. Most Bumiputra groups in peninsular Malaysia are known as Malay and are mostly Muslim by religion, though Sabah and Sarawak Bumiputra groups can be Muslim or non-Muslim.

periods, lack of performance monitoring and being internationally uncompetitive (Jomo & Wee, 2014). However, the heavy industrialisation programme was a 'push factor' to shift into technological-intensive activity. The programme also facilitated the creation of various domestic enterprises engaged in heavy industry.

The government continues to promote EOI under the Industrial Master Plan (IMP) versions I, II, and III. IMP I (1986–1996) provided a long-term development framework for resource and non-resource based industries. It further promoted export manufacturing sectors with an emphasis on technological deepening and human resource development. Various incentives and programmes were introduced such as the Promotion Investment Act 1986, the Intensification of Research Priority Areas programme, the Technological Action Plan and the Industrial Technical Assistance Fund (Tan, 2014). This saw rapid expansion of manufacturing exports, and at its peak Malaysia became one of the largest exporters of manufacturing products (especially in the E&E sector) in Southeast Asia (Lall, 1995). The average growth rate of the GDP during the 1990s was 7.4 per cent, which was the highest the country ever achieved (Hill, 2012) before the Asian Financial Crisis in 1997. While expansion of exports is commendable, lower local contents fell short in moving up into higher value-added sectors, which shows the lack of industrial upgrading (Tan, 2014). Therefore, with IMP II (1996–2006) the government further emphasised technological upgrading by building linkages, R&D activities and infrastructure development. IMP II also emphasised a cluster-based manufacturing strategy to strengthen industrial development, including heavy industry and particularly automotive sectors.

Against the backdrop of the global competitions and pressure from emerging markets, IMP III (2006–2020) emphasises industrial catch-up into mature broad-based manufacturing activities and innovative and competitive sectors (MITI, 2006). This is due to slowed productivity levels associated with the lack of technological upscaling and relatively lower level of skilled workers (Rasiah, 2011a, b). Industrial policy thus focuses on gearing towards global competitiveness by moving up the global value chain, with emphasis on value-added and knowledge-intensive activity. This signifies the government continues to focus on rapid structural change in heavy industrial sectors to graduate into higher technological activities. In 2006, regional economic corridors were introduced as part of the strategy to enhance industrial development. This is one of the integrated frameworks of industrial development within a specific geographical area that places trade- related infrastructure at the core (Athukorala & Narayan, 2017). The integrated framework attempts to utilise regional advantage such infrastructure, logistics, port facilities and resources. This designated geographical area intended to improve the investment climate while taking advantage of the regional production network. There are five economic corridors namely, (i) East Coast Economic Region (ii) Northern Corridor Economic Region (iii) Iskandar Malaysia (iv) Sarawak Corridor of Renewable Energy (v) Sabah Development Corridor. All these corridors have it owns strategic focus and to compliment every economic corridor. The economic corridors can provide enabling environment for foreign and local private sector initiative to promote industries along with government incentives. Setting up the regional corridors enable to promote entrepreneurial capabilities, support public–private partnership (PPP), facilitate the movement of labour across (based on specific skills) the regions, and promoting industrial clusters. Having industrial cluster also attempts to reap the benefits of reduced transport costs, shared inputs, and productivity spillover from learning and technology transfer (Athukorala & Narayan, 2017). This also helps improving the value chain so private firms can be more competitive. Overall corridors can help to 'pull the rest of the economy' driven by industrial based activities.

1.2 The Case Focus: Malaysia Automotive Industry

Automotive industry is one of the key primary sectors chosen under the heavy industrialisation program to spur industrial development. It is coined as 'industry of the industries' (Dicken, 2007) because the automotive industry involves complex products, with more than 3,000 parts and components that involve different production processes and considerable specialisation (Abdulsomad, 2003). Given that the industry has the potential to drive industrialisation from its spillover effect on other sectors (Dicken, 2007), the government sees the automotive industry as having strong relationships with economic development, generating employment, technological advancement and the hastening of the industrialisation process, hence improving the standard of living of the country. To date, the automotive industry has become one of the main key engines of growth for manufacturing in Malaysia. The industry has contributed RM50 billion (USD12.50 billion) or 4.9 per cent to the national GDP

Automotive industry is nothing new in Malaysia, this industry already began since in the 1960s and has become part of the global automotive production network ever since (Abdulsomad, 2003). The country adopted an import substitute industrialisation (ISI) strategy in automotive industries to spur industrialisation. ISI is typical approach to most developing countries to enhance industrial accumulation prior to twenty-first century. The complex production processes in automotive assembly hoped would enhance and diversify domestic manufacturing sectors such plastics, electronics, glass, steel and other metals, which could be linked up to the automotive production network. Foreign automakers were expected to contribute to the domestic economy in terms of technology advancement, skill development, and training and creation of small and medium enterprises (Abdulsomad, 1999, p. 274).

During the early 1960s, local content policy (localisation policy) was introduced as part of the policy instrument for ISI. Localisation policy intends to link local assemblers with foreign automakers. To this end the government imposes import restriction through manufacturing license and approve permits. Furthermore the government can provide grant or subsidies to help the local assemblers to grow in the automotive industry. Next, local content policy can foster 'learning by doing' to acquire skills for the local assemblers, so that they can increase their skills and move up in the automotive production chain. The government started to promote the imports for completely knocked-down (CKDs) items while restricting the imports of completely built units (CBUs). The restriction entails a complex import process, high import duty and quantitative restriction for CBUs.

In 1967, the first assembly plant, Swedish Motor Assemblies (a joint collaboration with Volvo) started to operate in Malaysia. In the same year, the government passed the Investment Incentive Act to encourage more assembly car manufacturers to use local parts. By the end of 1970s there were 11 assembly plants in Malaysia which produced 122 models of 25 makes of passenger cars and commercial vehicles (Athukorala, 2014). Companies involved in the car-assembly activities were Fiat, Mitsubishi, Chrysler, Volvo, Honda, Peugeot, Mercedes Benz, Toyota, Daihatsu, Fords, Land Rover and Citroen. Most of these foreign car companies engaged in assembly activities through equity and technical linkages with Malaysian local parts and components manufacturers who were mainly Chinese, and a small number who were Bumiputra (Jayasankaran, 1994; Jomo; 1983). Many of these firms began manufacturing replacement parts and intended to expand into the original equipment market (OEM) to supply local assemblers.

Most assembling processes focused on low-tier assembling functions such as installing tyres, batteries, dashboards, paint, filters, seat-belts and glass items. The government implemented a mandatory local content increase starting from 10 per cent in 1972 to 35 per cent in 1982, and protection for parts producers (Lim & Onn, 1983). The increase of local content was based on the Walker Report in 1970 that recommended an expansion of local content to 40 per cent over the next ten years (Lim & Onn 1983). The localisation policy was also in line with the New Economic Policy of 1970, which intended to increase Bumiputra participation in economic development. The localisation policy was to provide business opportunity for Bumiputra to partake in the auto industry, as previously there was little presence in the sector.

However, the first attempt to further increase the localisation program came with resistance from foreign investors. First, the cost of locally assembled parts was high because there was limited supply for components and parts available in the country. Most of the parts had to be imported from abroad, which increased the cost due to import duties. Second, the foreign companies, especially the Japanese, resisted compliance with the localisation program because the same price charged in Malaysia and Japan for the parts and components deleted in CKDs (Chan, 1988). The localisation program had negligible effect in the auto industry because of the abovementioned reasons. Furthermore, the problem with the localisation policy was that different manufacturers and cars needed various components, so the local manufacturers were unable to engage in mass production of parts and components. It was difficult for the local manufacturers to achieve economies of scales, hence did not give them price advantage (Tai & Ku, 2013).

In 1979, the government announced a mandatory deletion program (MDP) for CKDs. This program involved prohibition of some components in the CKDs from the approval lists, depending on local availability as agreed upon by foreign and local assemblers. The mandatory deletion program was supported by a strong protective measure for local producers such as incentives, tariff protections for parts producers and duty exemptions. The policy created market opportunity for local parts producers as well as for the Bumiputra community who were involved in the auto industry. There were approximately 200 parts and components producers and the level increased to

20 percent in 1980s (Chan, 1988; Lim & Onn, 1983). Later, the government adopted the Local Material Content Policy (LCMP) in 1992 that required an increase of local content between 45 and 60 percent (later it was phased out after Malaysia committed to WTO rules for liberalisation in the automotive industry in 2002 and onwards).

In the midst of 1980s under the Prime Minister Mahathir Mohammad (1981–2003) tenure, his administration made a bold move to introduce national car projects, namely Proton in 1985 and Perodua in 1994 under the heavy industrialisation programme. The program is in line with the Look East Policy which was inspired by the Northeast Asian industrial policy. Industrialising the country through building the local automotive industry is part of the government strategy to develop indigenous technological capabilities and upscaling the manufacturing activities (Jomo, 2007; Abdulsomad, 2003). It is part of the strategy to rationalise the automotive market previously dominated by foreign automakers (Abdulsomad, 1999). The national car projects also further create and strengthen local parts and components manufacturers. At the same time it pursues the government agenda of 'industrial nationalism' (Wad & Govindaraju, 2011) to enable the domestic automotive enterprises to lead manufacturing activities with little dependence on foreign companies. The heavy industrialisation programme also linked to the formation of Bumiputra industrial groups (Embong, 1996; Tan, 2008).

After the formation of national car projects the government employed selective interventions with heavy protection through tariff barriers and non-tariff barriers. This it to enable the infant industry to grow despite being considered a sunset industry at the time (Smith, 1994). Various programmes were introduced to facilitate the growth of the national carmaker, including a localisation policy and vendor development programmes (to nurture entrepreneurial skills for Bumiputra SME in the automotive production network) (Rosli & Kari, 2008; Alavi, 1996; 1999). The made-in-Malaysia car—Proton and, later, Perodua—dominates the domestic automotive market which was previously controlled by Japanese auto companies.

Over the years, Malaysia's automotive industry has come under the pressure of liberalisation, especially after the country became a member of WTO in 1995 and made the commitment to Common Effective Preferential Tariff (CEPT) in 2002 under the ASEAN free trade agreement (AFTA) (Athukorala, 2014). The government is acquiesced to open up the domestic automotive industry due to the presence of national cars. However the automotive industry could not operate in close environment in order to make the industry competitive. So in response to the liberalisation pressure, the government introduced Nationa Automotive Policy (NAP) 2006. The NAP is also one of the policy thrusts of the third Industrial Master Plan (IMP III 2006–2020) meant to achieve an 'industrialised nation' status in line with the 'Vision 2020' agenda. The NAP sets the country's strategic priorities and long-term developmental goals for the national automotive industry. The overarching goal is to liberalise the domestic automotive industry to improve the capability and competitiveness of the automotive industry in the ASEAN region and in global production (NAP, 2014)

The policy acknowledges the problems of the domestic automotive industry, including lack of economies of scale, high production costs, lack of technological upgrading and knowledge application, non-optimised supply chains and lack of development of human capital. The policy attempts to increase competitiveness in order to address structural problems (NAP, 2014, p. 5). The policy also advocates a transformative strategy for the national carmakers to be competitive in global automotive production. The policy puts special emphasis on the flagship Malaysia carmaker, Proton, though Proton has been labelled a huge liability due to its poor export performance, shrinking sales volumes and poor technological innovation (Rasiah, 2009; Kim, 2009). Foreign partnership is among others considerations to improve the national car performances. In 2017, Zhejiang Geely acquired 49.9 per cent of Proton's share, the Chinese company is also main stakeholder of Volvo and the third largest car manufacturer in China. This partnership agreement plan to improve export performance, technology advancement and utilise the production capacity. This first collaboration is to design a new and first Proton SUV based on the Geely Boyue model.

Latest development after Malaysia 14th General Election in 2018, which saw Pakatan Harapan led by Mahathir ousted the ailing Barisan Nasional, Mahathir who is currently the Prime Minister agreed to launch the 'Third National Car' under the new NAP 2020. Though this third national car plan has limited details, but according to the Prime Minister the third national car project will be a private initiative and no government intervention. The project will be headed by Malaysian company DreamEDGE Sdn Bhd and technologically backed by Daihatsu Motor Co Ltd. In NAP 2020, the focus on automotive industry emphasis on Next Generation Vehicle, Mobility as a Service and Industrial Revolution 4.0. While Energy Efficient Vehicle was one of the main theme of NAP 2014, but against the backdrop of digital industrial development, NAP 2020 attempt to move beyond EEV, while putting emphasis on research and development particularly on autonomous vehicle, electrification, Data Analytics, Internet of Things and Artificial Intelligence (AI) and alternative fuel powertrains.

The NAP 2020 reiterates the importance of investment, market expansion and moving up the value chain for automotive industry. This requires a more open automotive market. Despite Malaysia's commitments promoting a market-based economy in automotive industry, the government has not necessarily 'rolled back'. Though the NAP's purpose was to structure a business-friendly environment, the extent to which it is market friendly remains debatable. Given the government have substantial interest in the national car projects and that it is linked to ethnic development, it is logical to argue that the government would facilitate the national carmakers (this includes Bumiputra vendors) beyond an arm's length relationship against the backdrop of pro-market reforms. Particularly, Proton is characterised as a 'national interest' that continues to depend on government financial support (Tong et al., 2012). Such substantial interest means that liberalisation initiative is not done in liner way. Instead, the national automotive policy is coordinated by policy actors to protect the domestic automotive sectors (Mahidin & Kanageswary, 2004; Doner & Wad, 2014).

The formation of the NAP 2006 is considered to be the Malaysian government's initial pro-market reform to enhance competitiveness. In this sense, a freer marketplace is expected along with removal of trade barriers (MITI, 2014; Natsuda et al., 2013; Segawa et al, 2014; Natsuda & Thoburn, 2014). However, whenever the state interest is accounted for in industrial development, it creates a political economic dynamic in the policy-making process wherein state elites and their 'selected' private enterprise alliances attempt to preserve their interest (Whitfield & Therkildsen, 2011). It is obvious liberalisation can undermine the growth of the national car company. In this sense opening up the market is not feasible because it can undermine domestic enterprise and ethno-nationalist interest. On the other hand, having a close environment will not foster competitiveness in the automotive industry. Therefore, understanding the NAP requires exploration of the political economy of the Malaysia's industrial policy-making between policymakers. Using National Automotive Policy as case study enables an in-depth empirical investigation and analysis of the institutional arrangements made by the economic actors in Malaysia.

1.3 Rationale of the Study

Introduction of a heavy industrialisation programme by Prime Minister Mahathir Mohammad is one of the turning points for Malaysian economic policy (Jomo, 2007; Rasiah, 2011b). The heavy industrialisation programme marked the state adopts developmentalist state approach. Briefly, such an approach is one in which the state puts economic development as its top priority and industrial policy is devised to attain developmental goals (Embong, 2015; Bagchi, 2006). The programme aims at deepening and diversifying industrial structure through building linkages and developing indigenous technology capabilities, particularly in the automotive sector. Though the state adopts market liberalism, the presence of industrial policy (like the national automotive policy) means the state continues to have protective measures. The political economy of the industrial policy may appear to create a 'market friendly environment', but policy formulation is also designed to favour domestic enterprise (Lall, 1995; Embong, 2015).

Although heavy industry (using automotive sectors) was intended to diversify and strengthen the country's industrial base, politically, the programme was part of a nationalist economic project (Lim, 1994). The underlying purpose was to allow Bumiputra to lead industrial development and allow for the creation of a Bumiputra Commercial and Industry Community (BCIC) (Embong, 1996, p. 58). This 'ethnic imperative' is part of New Economic Policy objectives, therefore, the Bumiputra agenda is a significant part of the economic policy-making process. The NEP has formed a policy legacy for 'guiding principles' in Malaysia's economic policy (Menon, 2008).

In this sense, the formation of automotive sector cannot be separated from politics. Policy formation and implementation largely coincide with political interests and economic considerations. These two sets of interests tend to intertwine between state actors: on one hand, to preserve the Bumiputra class interest, meaning the state requires a certain degree of economic control over the marketplace. On the other, industrialising the country requires a market-friendly environment (liberalisation) to create a competitive economy. Often there is an economic efficiency trade-off when economic development is embedded with political considerations (Tan, 2015). However, this does not mean industrial development is not attainable. In fact, the strategic role of the state in Malaysia is to transform industrial structures, revealing the institutional capacity of the ruling elite in policy-making institutions to formulate and implement industrial policy (Smogyi, 1991; Bowie, 1991).

Industrial policy in Malaysia reveals the ability of the state to impose its will to achieve economic transformation. The ability of the state to impose its will is subject to the capacity of political institutions and the bureaucracy to express their industrial preferences in policy making (Haggard, 1998, p. 78). However, this capacity does not exist in a vacuum because economic transformation is grounded in the state and society mobilising resources. The ability of state actors to shift resources into heavy industry raises several questions: How are policy actors autonomous? How are power relations structured between state and society? How does this happen? Why are certain industrial sectors preferred over others? These questions are subject to the specific context of the domestic institutions (Brodsgaard & Young, 2000). Therefore, this requires a closer look at the political economy of industrial policy-making processes in Malaysia, where history, power relations, political processes and normative aspects influence policy formation.

This research aims to explore the political economy of Malaysia's industrial policy-making process. However, there is scant attention in Malaysian literature on the political economy of industrial policy, particularly the role of institutions (Doner, 1992; Doner & Ramsay, 2003; Leigh, 1992). Most discussion of industrial policy focuses on analysis of the policy outcome with neo-classical perspectives (Alavi, 1996; Lall, 1995). Analysis of policy also leans towards quantitative measures (Rasiah, 2011b; Tham, 2004; Mat Zin & Shahdan, 2009; Athukorala, 2004, 2010). This does not give deep insight into the political and economic reality of policy-making institutions. There is limited analysis of what takes place 'behind the scenes'. These limits provide the motivation to understand the political economy of policy-making institutions in Malaysia, specifically relating to national automotive policy, which forms a crucial part of the heavy industrialisation programme.

Most research in the area of the political economy of industrial policy making in Malaysia focuses on a developmentalist state approach (Embong, 1995; Abbott, 2003), an ethnic approach (Jesudason, 1989; Hirschman, 1986; Brennan, 1982), class-based analysis (Jomo, 1986; Lim & Canak, 1981; Lim, 1985), patronage in economic policy (Gomez & Jomo, 1997), rent-seeking (Searle, 1999; Tan, 2008; Khan, 2000) and leadership and policy making (Leong, 1992; Milne & Mauzy, 1999). Such scholarly work has contributed valuable insights into the politics of industrial policy using different theoretical lenses. However, there has been less attention paid to the role of institutions in policy making (Aun, 2002; Tipton, 2009). Linder and Peter (1990) argue that institutions seldom play a distinct role in policy making, when in fact institutions shape capacity, belief systems, preferences and interactions that facilitate or constrain policy processes. The presence of the patronage system, rent-seeking behaviour, the dominant role of elites in policy institutions and the nexus of ties between the state and market all exist because of the domestic institutions that enable and support such interactions.

Pertinent to Malaysia's institutional context, the institutions enable the political elite, bureaucracy and other economic agents, the capacity to define industrial preferences in policy-making. Hence, elite policy actors can prescribe and guide the decisions and actions of policy makers to realise industrial policy (Felker, 1999; Aun, 2002). This also sets the boundaries of interactions between economic actors, including how the state elites and industrial groups 'get things done' by advancing their political and economic interests in the institutions they are embedded in. This analysis intends to bring institutions to the forefront in analysing the political economy of industrial policy formation. Furthermore, there is a need to focus on the institutional arrangements between policy actors. Institutional arrangements that are part of the coordination of policy making are subject to wider institutional constraints (for example, power relations and historical events). Such constraints also shape how policy actors advance their preferences in policy institutions (Fox & Miller, 1995). The coordination of policy-making has to pay close attention to the relationship between state elites (politicians and bureaucrats) and selected business groups. This research will explore in detail the 'triangular arrangement' of those elite policy actors in configuring policy interests. Interaction of these actors will highlight the dynamic of politics and economic policy making institutions in Malaysia.

1.4 Book Structure

Following this introduction, chapter Two discusses the theoretical foundation of this research. The theories of new institutionalism and a developmental state approach are presented. The identified theoretical themes are then integrated and developed as a theoretical framework used to explain, analyse and make sense of the political economy of the policy-making process in Malaysia. In this chapter 'triangular arrangement' will be formulated using new institutional theory and developmental state approach as theoretical frame to understand the institutional arrangements between policy-makers in Malaysia. Chapter 2 also includes discussion the methodology employs in this study. The study uses qualitative research methods to analyse dynamic of political economy of industrial policy on automotive industries. Primary data are collected from key policy makers such as senior politicians, high level civil servants, heads of corporate and business association, prominent political economists and economists. Chapter 3 discusses the significance of the heavy industrialisation programme that gave birth to the national car project. It is an ambitious project that marked the state's adoption of a developmentalist state approach in pursuit of 'national champion'. This follows by assessment of the protectionist measures formed by the state to protect the domestic automotive industry. Discussion also includes the pressure for liberalisation in automotive sector and the formation of National Automotive Policy as a response to the pro-market reforms. Chapter 4 discusses the national car project and the national automotive policy being geared towards full-fledged car manufacturers facilitated by the role of institutions. This chapter examines the politics of Proton as the flagship of the national car manufacturers, which further reveals the strategic role of the political elite in facilitating the growth of Proton and also constraining factors. Chapter 5 presents an assessment of political economy of national automotive Industry. First section will analyse the role of political institutions defining and defending the interest of automotive industry. This follows by assessment of government-business relationship reveal how institutional arrangements are made between the government and industrial groups to secure the interest of domestic enterprise in the automotive industry against the backdrop of pro-market reforms. Next the role of bureaucracy in national automotive policy, this section highlights the strong politico-bureaucratic ties enable the political elite to impose its will onto the state agencies. This made the pilot agencies who responsible for industrial planning adjust policy terms in favour of the domestic enterprise, despite how it may affect the overall efficiency of the automotive industry. The overall analysis here represents the role of institutions in facilitating and constraining actors in the policy-making institutions. The triangular arrangement (formal or informal) between the political elite, bureaucracy and 'selected' private enterprises can change aspects of policy or prevent coherent national automotive policy implementation. Finally, chapter six provides an overall discussion of the topic based on the data analysis. This chapter presents what can be learnt from the findings of the politics of industrial policy-making process in Malaysia. This chapter will highlight the pressing issues that hinder the growth of Malaysia automotive industry. Suggestion to overcome the problems are also discussed. The final chapter also summarises the overall findings and provides an outlook for further research in the areas industrial policy.

References

Abdulsomad, K. (1999). Promoting industrial and technological development under contrasting industrial policies: The automotive industry in Malaysia and Thailand. In K. S. Jomo, G. Felker, & R. Rasiah (Eds.), *Industrial technology development in Malaysia: Industry and firm studies*. New York, NY: Routledge.

Abdulsomad, K. (2003). Building technological capabilities of local auto parts firms under contrasting industrial policies: A comparative study of Malaysia and Thailand 1960–2000. In *Lund Studies in Economic History*. Lund University.

Abbott, J. (2003). *Developmentalism and dependency in Southeast Asia*. London: Routledge.

Alavi, R. (1996). *Industrialisation in Malaysia: Import substitution and infant industry performance*. London: Routledge.

Alavi, R. (1999). Rents, technological innovation and firm competitiveness in a Bumiputra Malaysian firm. In K. S. Jomo, G. Felker, & R. Rasiah (Eds.), *Industrial technology development in Malaysia: Industry and firm studies*. London: Routledge.

Athukorala, P. C. (2004). *Trade policy issues in Asian development*. London: Routledge.

Athukorala, P. C. (2010). *Production network and trade pattern in East Asia: Regionalisation and globalisation?* Asian Development Bank.

Athukorala, P. C. (2014). *Industrialisation through state-MNC partnership: Lesson from Malaysia national car project* (Working Paper No. 2014/06). Arndt-Corden Department of Economics, Crawford School of Public Policy.

Athukorala, P. C., & Narayan, S. (2017). *Economic corridors and regional development: The Malaysian experience* (Asian Development Bank Economics Working Paper Series).

Aun, L. H. (2002). *Industrial development and equity distribution in Malaysia manufacturing: Institutional perspectives* (Working Paper Series Centre on Regulation and Competition). University of Manchester.

Bagchi, A. K. (2006). The developmental state under imperialism. In K. S. Jomo (Ed.), *The long twentieth century: Globalization under hegemony*. New Delhi: Oxford University Press.

Bowie, A. (1991). *Crossing the industrial divide: State, society and the politics of economic transformation in Malaysia*. New York, NY: Columbia University Press.

Brennan, M. (1982). Class, politics and race in modern Malaysia. *Journal of Contemporary Asia, 12*, 188–215.

Brodsgaard, K. E., &Young, S. (2000). Introduction: State capacity in East Asia. In K. E. Brodsgaard & S. Young (Eds.), *State capacity in East Asia: Japan, Taiwan, China, and Vietnam*. New York, NY: Oxford University Press.

Chan, P. (1988). Economic regulations in Malaysia with reference to motor vehicle and components industry. In R. F. Doner (Ed.), *The Dilemma and limits of state autonomy in Malaysia: The case of national car project*.

Dicken, P. (2007). *Global shift: Mapping the changing contours of the world economy*. New York, NY: The Guilford Press.

Doner, F. R., & Wad, P. (2014). Financial crisis and automotive industry development in Southeast Asia. *Journal of Contemporary Asia, 44*(4), 664–687.

Doner, R. F. (1992). Limits of state strength: Toward an institutionalist view of economic development. *World Politics, 44*(3), 398–431.

Doner, R. F., & Ramsay, A. (2003). The challenges of economics upgrading in liberalising Thailand. In L. Weiss (Ed.), *State in the global economy*. Cambridge University Press.

Embong, A. R. (1995). Social transformation, the state and the middle classes in post-independence Malaysia. *Southeast Asia Studies, 34*(3).

Embong, A. R. (1996). Social transformation, the state and the middle classes in post-independence Malaysia. *Southeast Asia Studies, 34*(3).

Embong, A. R. (2015). Developmentalist state in Malaysia: Its origins, nature and contemporary transformation. In J. M. Nelson, J. Meerman, & A. R. Embong (Eds.), *Globalisation and national autonomy: The experience of Malaysia*. Singapore: Institute of Southeast Asian Studies (ISEAS).

Felker, G. (1999). Malaysia innovation system: Actor, interest and governance technology, competitiveness and the state Malaysia industrial technology policies. In G. Felker & K. S. Jomo (Eds.), *Technology, competitiveness and the state: Malaysia's industrial technology policies*. London: Routledge.

Fox, C., & Miller, H. (1995). *Postmodern public administration*. Thousand Oaks, CA: Sage.

Gomez, E. T., & Jomo, K. S. (1997). *Malaysia's political economy: Politics, patronage and profits*. Cambridge: Cambridge University Press.

Haggard, S. (1998). Business, politics and policy in East and Southeast Asia. In S. R. Henry (Ed.), *Behind East Asia growth: The political and social foundations of prosperity*. London: Routledge.

Hill, H. (2012). *Malaysia economic development: Looking backwards and forward* (Working Paper No. 2010/13). Arndt Corden Department of Economics Crawford School of Economics and Government ANU College of Asia and the Pacific.

Hirschman, C. (1986). The making of race in colonial Malaya: Political economy and racial ideology. *The Eastern Sociological Society, 1*(2), 330–361.

Jayasankaran, S. (1994). Made in Malaysia: The Proton project. In K. S. Jomo (Ed.), *Japan and Malaysian development—In the shadow of the rising sun*. London: Routledge.

Jesudason, J. V. (1989). *Ethnicity and the economy: State, Chinese Business and Multinational in Malaysia*. Singapore: Oxford University Press.

Jomo, K. S. (1983). Project Proton: Malaysian car, Mitsubishi profits. In K. S. Jomo (Ed.), *The sun also set*. Institute of International Affairs.

Jomo, K. S. (1986). *A question of class: Capital, the state, and uneven development in Malaya.* Singapore and New York, NY: Oxford University Press.

Jomo, K. S. (2007). Industrialisation and industrial policy in Malaysia. In K. S. Jomo (Ed.), *Malaysia industrial policy.* Singapore: NUS press.

Jomo, K. S. (Ed.). (1993). *Industrializing Malaysia: Policy, performance, prospects.* Routledge

Jomo, K. S., & Edward, C. (1993). Malaysian industrialisation in historical perspective. In K. S. Jomo (Ed.), *Industrializing Malaysia: Policy, performance, prospects.* Routledge.

Jomo, K. S., & Wee, C. H. (2014). *Malaysia@50: Economic development, distribution and disparaties.* Strategic Information and Research Development Malaysia.

Khan, M. (2000). Rents, rent-seeking and economic development: An introduction. In M. Khan (Ed.), *Rent, rent-seeking and economic development: Theory and evidence in Asia.* Cambridge University Press.

Kim, W. (2009). Rethinking colonialism and the origins of the developmental state in East Asia. *Journal of Contemporary Asia, 39,* 382–399.

Lall, S. (1995). Malaysia: Industrial success and the role of the government. *Journal of International Development, 7*(5), 759–773.

Leigh, M. (1992). Politics, bureaucracy and business in Malaysia: Realigning the eternal triangle. In M. Andrew & J. Kanishka (Eds.), *The dynamics of economic policy reforms in Southeast Asia and the Southwest Pacific.* Singapore: Oxford University Press.

Leong, H. K (1992). Dynamic of policy making in Malaysia: The formulation of the new economic policy and the national development policy. *Asian Journal of Public Administration, 14*(2), 204–227.

Lim, C. P. (1994). Heavy industrialisation: A second round of import substitution. In K. S. Jomo (Ed.), *Japan and Malaysian development—In the shadow of the rising sun.* London: Routledge.

Lim, C. P., & Onn, F. C. (1983). Ancillary firm development in the Malaysia motor vehicle industry. In K. Odaka (Ed.), *The motor vehicle industry in Asia: A study of ancillary firm development.* University Singapore Press.

Lim, H. M., & Canak, W. (1981). The political economy of state policies in Malaysia. *Journal of Contemporary Asia, 11,* 208–224.

Lim, M. H. (1985). Contradictions in the development of Malay capital: State, accumulation and legitimation. *Journal of Contemporary Asia, 15*(1).

Linder, S. H., & Peter, G. B. (1990). An institutional approach to the theory of policy making: The role of guidance mechanism in policy formulation. *Journal of Theoretical Politics, 2*(1), 59–83.

Mahidin, M. U., & Kanageswary, R. (2004). The development of automotive industry and the road ahead. *Journal of Department of Statistic Malaysia, 2,* 1–32.

Mat Zin, R., & Shahdan, F. (2009). *Impact of global economic crisis on the Malaysian auto-parts industry.* Asian Development Bank.

Menon, J. (2008). *Macroeconomic management amid ethnic diversity: Fifty years of Malaysian experience* (ADB Institute Discussion Paper No. 102).

Milne, R., & Mauzy, D. (1999). *Malaysian politics under Mahathir.* London: Routledge.

Ministry of International Trade and Industry (MITI). (2006). *Third industrial master plan.* http://www.miti.gov.my/miti/resources/fileupload/contents.pdf.

Ministry of International Trade and Industry Malaysia (MITI). (2014). *Review of national automotive policy: MITI advances the Government of Malaysia's agenda of liberalisation, paving the way for a more competitive automotive industry for domestic, regional and global markets.* http://www.miti.gov.my/index.php/pages/view/1449.

National Automotive Policy (NAP). (2014). http://www.maa.org.my/pdf/NAP_2014_policy.pdf.

Natsuda, K., & Thoburn, J. (2014). How much policy space still exists under the WTO? A comparative study of the automotive industry in Thailand and Malaysia. *Review of International Political Economy, 21*(6), 1346–1377.

Natsuda, K., Segawa, N., & Thoburn, J. (2013). Globalisation and the Malaysia automotive industry: Industrial nationalism, liberalisation and the role of Japan. *Global Economic Review*, 42(2).

Rasiah, R. (2009). Technological capabilities of automotive firms in Indonesia and Malaysia. *Asian Economic Paper, 8*(1).
Rasiah, R. (2011a). *Industrialization and export-led growth In Malaysia: Policies and issues in economic development*. Kuala Lumpur: Institute of Strategic and International Studies (ISIS) Malaysia.
Rasiah, R. (2011b). Industrial policy and industrialization. In R. Rasiah (Ed.), *Malaysian economy: Unfolding growth and social change*. Kuala Lumpur: Oxford University Press.
Rasiah, R., & Shari, I. (2001). Market, government and Malaysia's new economic policy. *Cambridge Journal of Economics, 25*, 57–78.
Rosli, M., & Kari, F. (2008). *The comparative performance of local and foreign suppliers in the Malaysian automotive industry: The case of Proton's vendor*. Paper presented at the International Conference on Foreign Direct Investment and Technology Transfer in Asia, AEI/UM, Kuala Lumpur, Malaysia.
Searle, P. (1999). *The riddle of Malaysia capitalism*. Allen and Unwin: Crows Nest, NSW.
Segawa, N., Natsuda, K., & Thoburn, J. (2014). Affirmative action and economic liberalisation: The dilemmas of the Malaysian automotive industry. *Asian Studies Review, 38*(3), 422–441.
Smith, W. A. (1994). A Japanese factory in Malaysia: Ethnicity as a management ideology. In K. S. Jomo (Ed.), *Japan and Malaysian development—In the shadow of the rising sun*. London: Routledge.
Smogyi, J. (1991). Malaysia's successful reform experience. *Finance and Development*.
Tai, W. P., & Ku, S. C. Y. (2013). State and industrial policy: Comparative political economic analysis of automotive industrial policies in Malaysia and Thailand. *Journal of ASEAN, 1*(1), 55–82.
Tan, J. (2008). *Privatisation in Malaysia: Regulation, rent-seeking and policy failure*. Routledge.
Tan, J. (2014). Running out of steam? Manufacturing in Malaysia. *Cambridge Journal of Economics, 38*, 153–180.
Tan, J. (2015). Rent seeking and money politics in Malaysia: Ethnicity, cronyism and class. In W. Meredith (Ed.), *Routledge Handbook of contemporary Malaysia*. New York, NY: Routledge.
Tham, S. Y. (2004) The future of industrialisation in Malaysia under WTO. *Asia pacific Development Journal, 11*(1).
Tipton, F. B. (2009). *Southeast Asian capitalism: History, institutions, states, and firms*. Asia Pacific Journal of Management.
Tong, J. T., Terspstra, R. H., & N.C. Lim. (2012). Proton: Its rise, fall and future perspectives. *Asian Case Research Journal, 16*(2).
Wad, P., & Govindaraju, C. V. G. R. (2011). Automotive industry in Malaysia: An assessment of its development. *International Journal Automotive Technology and Management, 11*(2), 152–171.
Whitfield, L., & Therkildsen, O. (2011). *What drives state to support the development of productive sectors? Strategies ruling elites pursue political survival and their policy implication*.

Chapter 2
Theoretical Framework

2.1 The Role of Institutions

This research will view the role of institutions from the theoretical lenses of historical and sociological institutionalism. Linking the historical and sociological, on one hand, the aim is to understand that actors' behaviour is institutionally bounded, and their preferences are politically and socially constructed. On the other hand, the aim is to assess the normative and cognitive dimension. Incorporating both, it 'holds the centre' for institutional analysis and a more expansive view of the role of institutions. Therefore, it goes beyond strategic context to a set of shared understanding that affects the way problems are perceived and solutions are sought. The two approaches provide a 'context-specific' approach to a country's institutional design, as Thelen and Steinmo (1992) argue, 'provide[s] strong focus on how institutional structures politics yielded compelling accounts of policy continuities within countries over time and different policy outcome across countries'.

Historical institutionalism (HI) defines institutions as formal or informal procedures, routines, norms, standard operating procedures and conventions embedded in the organisational structures of the polity or political economy (Hall & Taylor, 1996, p. 938). It is a 'structural frame that constructs the relationship between actors in various units of polity and the economy' (Hall, 1986, p. 19). The important assumption here is that the rationality of actors is institutionally bounded (Braathen, 1996). Political actors are not so much all-knowing rational maximisers as they are rule-following satisfiers (March & Olsen, 1989). Actors' strategic choices are confined because choices are institutionally defined, and the pursuit of these choices may not always be as significant as actors think.

From the historical perspective, the state is conceptualised as a complex set of institutions that interacts between the social and political institutions. Institutionalist scholars within this paradigm take history seriously, as points out that 'history matters' because political decisions on certain policy take place within historical contexts, which has direct consequences on the institutional setting (Steinmo, 2008).

F. Suffian, *Political Economy of Malaysia's Industrial Policy*,
https://doi.org/10.1007/978-981-33-6901-6_2

The history of institutional design highlights the 'whole range of state and societal institutions that structure power relations between political actors and other actors embedded in the institutional context' (Thelen & Steinmo, 1992, p. 2). Consequently, the institutions determine distribution of power between political actors and other groups. This structure the interaction of political actors and their capacity to define and defend interests. The unintended consequence is that actors embedded in the institutions are subject to asymmetrical power relations (Hall & Taylor, 1996). Configuration of policy preferences and ideas in the political institutions are subject to uneven distribution of power between political elites and other social groups.

Sociological institutionalism (SI) defines institutions as the formal rules, procedures or norms, symbols system, cognitive scripts and moral templates that provide the 'frame of meaning' guiding human actions (Hall & Taylor, 1996, p. 947). Institutions is a social structure that are composed of regulative, normative and cultural cognitive elements that, together with associated activities and resources, provide stability and meaning to social life (Scott, 2001, p. 48). This paradigm is cultural-sensitive because proponents of this approach see blurred lines between institutions and cultures (Meyer, 2010; DiMaggio, 1998). This brings their emphasis to the normative and cognitive dimension (informal rules) (Hall & Taylor, 1996; Dobbin, 2004). The normative dimension refers to how institutions influence behaviours based on expected norms or shared values and understanding between individual actors. The cognitive dimension is based on the individual actors' responses and interpretation of meaning for action as structured by the institutions (Dimaggio & Powell, 1983).

Institutions are seen as rules that structure interaction between actors, affecting social, political and economic outcomes. Also known as 'rules of the game' in the society (North, 1991). The role of institutions focuses its interest on the interaction of polities (the political institutions) and politics (the political process) to explain policies (outcome) (Jenniver, 2009, p. 32). In relations to this, different countries have different institutional set-ups because formation of institutions broadly depends on the society' culture, habit and history. Institutions are linked to the path dependence, a collective decision in the past by a society on how things are done (Hall, 2001). Sewell (1996) points out that 'what has happened at an earlier point in time will affect the possible outcomes of a sequence of events occurring at a later time' (p. 262), which creates a historical legacy of rules, capacities and norms. Such legacy is an 'intergenerational transfer from past to present' (Beissinger & Young, 2002), and institutions transmit the norms, values, capacities and routines acquired in previous times (Jenniver, 2009, p. 38).

Institutions are linked to certain legacies, as Pierson argues, 'past line of policy condition subsequent policy by encouraging societal forces to organised along the same line than the others' (cited in Hall & Taylor, 1996, p. 941). The established legacy has a powerful effect on institutions for a long period of time, which structures individual behaviours, because once rules, norms and values are institutionalised, actors adapt their strategies in a way that reflects the institutions and reinforces the logic of systems across actors embedded in the institutions (Thelen, 1999). This can potentially constrain possibilities for change in policy, as Thelen claims that institutions are 'isomorphic' (compatible with resembling or renewing with similar logic), because political elites interpret based on the institutions they are embedded in, so even when the actors attempt to redesign institutions they are constrained in what they can conceive due to these embedded and cultural constraints (p. 386). North (1991) terms the situation as the 'locked in' effect of the institutions, and changes to institutions are often limited, especially as powerful actors that benefit from the institutional setting can constrain institutional change. This effect enables institutions to persist over time.

However, this does not mean institutional change does not take place. Institutional change is possible through 'critical junctures', moments when substantial institutional change can take place, thereby creating a new path from the historical development (Gourevitch, 1986). This happens when institutional arrangements take place and depends on collective actions attained by various actor groups in a society to create incentive for change (Hodgson, 1999). Changes can come from a 'shock' such as conflict or crisis, exogenous pressure (liberalisation) or the political process in policy field (Boettke et al., 2008). A 'shock' can lead to revolutionary change especially when there is a breakdown of institutions (Krasner, 1988). However, Thelen (2002) argues that not all environmental shifts are destabilising and not all shocks cause institutional breakdown. In fact, institutional change can be evolutionary because the need to change is always a question between beneficiaries and non-beneficiaries. The interplay of society and political power groups has decisive effects on institutional change to be evolutionary (Thelen, 1999). Therefore, new rules or governance can be formally introduced, but may not necessarily undermine informal institutions and powerful actors' interests in old institutions, so such change can be incremental.

Path dependence bears on institutional constraint for actors' interactions. An Institutional legacy can lead to a 'distributional effect,' referring to the role of power and asymmetrical relations of power plays between groups. Thelen (1999) points out that 'institutions are not neutral coordinating mechanisms but in fact reflect, and also reproduce and magnify, particular patterns of power distribution in politics' (p. 394). The distribution of power in political institutions makes a difference in policy outcome (March & Olsen, 1984), because institutions structure some groups (for example elites or interest groups) to have access to the decision-making process. Asymmetrical power relations provide certain groups of elites with an advantage over others. Elites here are individuals or groups (usually very few) who have power to shape main political and economic outcomes. Even though policy decision is open for competition between numerous groups, institutional constraints can circumscribe political participations and equality, hence can lead to unequal access to the decision-making process. Therefore, political institutions structure the kinds of interest most likely to be represented in the policy process (Steinmo, 1993).

An important assumption about the role of institutions is that political actors are not utility maximisers (abiding by rules to increase individual gain or maximise interest), they are utility 'satificers' (Braathen, 1996). Meaning actors are norm-abiding rule followers, meanwhile attempting to maximise their interests within the institutional context. So how one behaves depends on the individual, the context, time and rules. In other words, an actor will respond to what is appropriate behaviour within the broader cultural environment (Hall & Taylors, 1996, p. 949). In this sense, actors—institutions, in particular—seek to define and express a certain identity in socially appropriate ways (Hall & Taylor, 1996, p. 949). March and Olsen (1989) suggest that what is appropriate is also how political institutions define and interpret the world view, and respond to a particular situation based on the institutionalised norms, values and capacity. As such, actors behave strategically within the institutional context. As Steinmo (2008) (a proponent of historical institutionalism) argues, 'humans are not simple rule followers', while the role of institutions structures norms and rules, political actors operating in an institution will act strategically based on existing norms, values and rules (what is appropriate) to attain their interests, with a purpose of political stability (Jenniver, 2009). This has implications on spreading policy ideas and configuring preferences and interests, and hence influences policy outcome (Campbell, 1998).

The role of institutions can shape political and economic interest (Campbell & Pedersen, 2001). Historical institutionalist scholars define interest as 'the real, material interest of the principle actors whether conceived as individual or as groups' (Hall, 1997, p. 176). The role of institutions restricts certain sets of ideas which political elites find acceptable, and formal institutions mediate the degree to which elites transport different ideas into the policy-making domain for consideration (Campbell, 1998, p. 378). This suggests that to seek political solutions or resolve conflicts, political elites tend to favour their material interests (or groups associated with them) over other disadvantaged groups (Hall, 1997, p. 937). The balance of power between groups structures the capacity of them to channel interest in the policy making arenas. This is the reason why some ideas or preferences are considered, why certain ideas or interest are adopted, and why others are not. It is also why certain groups are able to advance their policy ideas, but others are not (Campbell, 1998; Thelen, 1999).

The role of institutions shape interpretations for possible courses of action by political elites. The interpretive frame of actors is deemed central to how the elite 'package' formation of policy interest to convince the general public that certain policy proposals constitute plausible and acceptable solutions to problems within the institutional context (Campbell, 1997, 1998). Institutions enable interests to be interpreted by political elites according to regulative and normative institutions, they are subject to constant manipulations by political actors to respond to specific situations and circumstances (Lewellen, 2003). Schattschneider (1957) points out that political organisation is the 'mobilisation of bias', where political actors have bias in favour of exploiting some kinds of interests while suppressing others. The role of institutions enables elites to interpret policy interest to prevent change in policy outcome or block potential policy that is against their interest. In this context, even though change takes place, it is subject to '*layering*': the creation of new rules together with old ones where change occurs not through the displacement of old rules, but rather through the addition of new ones on top of old ones. It can also occur through '*conversion*', where rules remain formally the same but become interpreted and enacted differently (Mahoney & Thelen, 2010, p. 17). This suggests that though there are well-established rules, the interpretation of them can act as a constraint on how a possible course of action is defined or framed. A leadership role is significant to define preferences based on the normative and cognitive dimension of the institutional setting.

Formal rules (codified rules) and informal institutions (norms, values) construct the role of institutions. Formal rules or the written code of conduct prescribed and proscribed actor's interactions and behaviours. As much as formal rules are seen straightforward to shape interactions and behaviours, but the informal institutions have a profound impact on shaping actors' interactions, preferences and objectives. The informal institutions institutionalised norms and embedded conventions (Scott, 2008). The informal institutions embody customs, tradition and code of conduct structures of behaviour, interaction and preferences. The normative dimension (the unwritten code of conduct) institutionalised certain norms that form a binding expectation for actors' behaviour. Institutionalised norms like standard operating procedure reflect the routine way in which people do what they are supposed to do (March & Olsen, 1989, p. 21). Scott also refers to the normative dimension as logic of appropriateness (drawing from Campbell's work), which usually refers to what is the appropriate behaviour one *should* do in accordance to the cultural context. In this sense, the informal institutions set a powerful course of social interaction in a given institutional context.

Informal institutions can act as sanctioning in social interaction because they institutionalised a standard of expected behaviour, so violated norms may lead to social disapproval or punishment as a way to discontinue the interactions. Helmke and Levitsky (2004) refer to 'informal institutions as socially shared rules, non-codified, communicated and enforced outside of officially sanctioned channels' (p. 727). They view informal institutions as important avenues for political actors to influence the political process. Basically, informal rules are the 'actual rules being followed' if the social interaction between actors in a particular institution includes rewards, for example, in a patron-client network (O'Donnell, 1996). These can be actual rules that structure interaction to advance individual interests, because informal mechanisms govern network-controlled exchanges and norms become the 'rules of the games' (Collin, 2002, p. 23). The informal dimension can have a critical part to play in maintaining, preventing or undermining consensus and adherence to formal rules (Leftwich, 2010, p. 7). It is also a powerful form of interaction in discussion or cooperation between economic actors and those who influence policy arrangement.

From the above discussion it is obvious that 'institutions matter' as they shape, facilitate and constrain actors' interactions. An important consideration of institutionalism is that there is no homogenous set of institutions because different societies have distinctive sets of rules, norms, values and embedded conventions. This manifests different institutional designs across countries, so the institutional design of developed countries could not be compared to that of developing countries. This is because institutions are embedded with historical specificities, unique norms and conventions. Hence the role of institutions will have implications on the policy making processes.

2.2 Developmental State and the Role of Institutions

The developmental state approach is commonly referred to regarding the late industrializing countries, particularly Northeast Asia (Japan, South Korea and Taiwan) and some Southeast Asia countries. Following the success of the Asian economy, industrial growth is seen as a country getting the 'right fundamental policy,' such as market-friendly economic policies to promote industrial development. The industrial accumulation of a late industrialising country could not merely be assessed from neo-classical perspectives (macroeconomic stability, enforcement of rules, high rate of physical and human capital investment, clear property rights), the state plays a strategic role to facilitate industrial development growth. This again challenges the description of neo-classical accounts on economic development.

The developmental state concept is referred to as the state seeks to attain economic development through industrialisation by improving targeted sectors to make them competitive at the international level (Johnson, 1999). The overarching intention is to promote long-term entrepreneurial perspectives among the industrial elite comprising key business groups and resist growth-compromising demands from special interest groups (Johnson, 1982; Evans, 1995 cited in Low, 2001 p. 413). The approach does not downplay the role of market institutions in the process of modernising the national economy. However, the state devises policy instruments embedded with national interest to guide the market. The state 'provides directional thrust to the operation of the market mechanism, and the market is guided by long term national rationality of investment formulated by the state's institutions. The role of institutions in such states enable the state elites and selective producers to deliberate policy, and thus can alter market incentives while protecting vested interests and creating obscurity (Low, 2001, p. 413).

The strategic role of the state intervening in the market for rapid industrial development becomes an overriding consideration in the developmental state (Onis, 1991). Scholars like Abbott (2004), Low (2004), Johnson (1982), Woo-Cumming (1999) and Henderson (1993) who observe the capitalist development of the developmental state suggest that the political economy of such states is described as *plan-rational*. In such economies, the state itself leads the industrialisation drive, taking on developmental functions (Johnson, 1982, p. 19). The state is able to set substantive social and economic goals. The government will give priority to the structure of domestic industry and promote the structure that enhances the nation's international competitiveness; hence this implies a strategic or goal-oriented approach, such as short-term or long-term industrial policy. Though the state plays strategic roles, the economy remains largely in the hands of private corporations, which exposes it to a market discipline environment (Abbott, 2003, p. 27). Though the state ensures rules are adhered to in the market economy, the institutional design of the developmental state structures an interwoven relationship between state and market. Therefore, the state would intervene where necessary in order to achieve national goals, including going beyond arm's length relationships to facilitate private enterprises.

The developmentalist state approach can structure its market entry and direct private companies' activities in selected industries. The national institutions enable the government to shape the market to support entry for new industries and encourage investment in a sector (Whitley, 1999). The existing state capacity of the developmental state provides institutional strength and the ability to exercise a large measure of control over the behaviour of domestic and foreign capital (Koo & Kim, 1992). Market entry for foreign direct investment is structured into certain industries that can build links with domestic industry (most of the Southeast Asian countries are unable to emulate this because the country's industrialisation depends on foreign direct investment). In the developmentalist state approach the state is also likely to be *selective*, meaning that the state tends to create progressively shifting competitive advantage instead of just adapting to existing comparative advantage (Lauridsen, 1995, p. 27). One example is the transformation from an agricultural based to industrial based economy, or effective industrial upgrading (from mid-tier function to innovative activities). When it shifts to certain industrial sectors, the government initiates most major investment for the private sector, and as such the state would ensure private sectors have access to state resources. Strategically shifting from one sector to another may give rise to a plausible tension regarding resources allocation. However, the state elites can resolve conflict (for instance between different segments of capital), then allocate resources to the most productive groups. Then, state elites can construct economic rules that advance long-term sectional interests, technological character and promote growth (Pempel, 1999).

In this sense, the developmental process is based on close connections between state and 'selected' industrial groups and is a conjoining effort to modernise the domestic economy (Woo-Cumming, 1999). Deliberations of economic strategy is devised by either formal or informal ways between government and private sectors. 'Numerous unusual institutional arrangements' take place to facilitate the growth of the private sector with preferential access to state resources (Johnson, 1982, p. 312; Abbott, 2004). Close ties between the state elites and industrial groups enable these actors to configure policy arrangements through deliberation to resolve conflict, determine preferences and adjust economic policy outcome. State elites can mobilise state resources swiftly, instead of relying on the market mechanism (Wade, 1990). The ongoing consultation enables the state to prioritise research and development, financial support, technological upgrading and training and development. The state elites are able mobilise resources from unproductive industrial groups to more productive ones, while imposing discipline through export performance, attaining greater economies of scale and improve the learning curve (playing industrial catch up) (Jomo, 2004, p. 59).

The close connection between government and industrial groups in the developmental state approach allows the state to produce coherent industrial policy. The ability of the state to shift resources to a particular industrial group reveals that the state has the ability to mobilise resources without being challenged by organised groups (trade union and civil society) or other private interest groups (landowner). Developmental states tend to have a weak social class. This affects the organisation of interest groups such as labour unions or civil society groups to form collective actions. Wade (1990) points out that the state does not sanction the creation of peak organisation entirely. To support policy formation, the state nurtures the formation of organised groups to advocate for the interests of the industrial groups linked to state elites. The organised groups are involved in the policy making process, but the extent to which these organised groups can have equal bargaining power between the state elites (politician, bureaucrats) and industrial groups remains limited (Onis, 1991).

The institutional environment where the state elites have weak links with societal groups enables the elites to prioritise rapid economic development and rising standard of living as means of providing legitimacy for the ruling elite. Dean's (2000) observation on capitalist developmental states describes this as *developmental legitimacy*, whereby development forms the most important legitimising principle of the state. The legitimacy of the state elites is based on developmental achievement, that is ability to promote and sustain development with combination of steady high rates of economic growth and structural change in productive system (Castell, 1992). It is when the state elites commit to economic transformation to improve the material needs of the society, so the people are committed to the economic order. This is likely to reduce the formation of collective interests among other groups to undermine elites' interest in pursuit of economic development. In the economic policy front, the elites are able to prioritise the need for economic development and steer away from unnecessary private interests of groups that can compromise the implementation of economic policy (Abbott, 2003, 2004).

Developmental states the state ideology is important and can provide powerful tools for ruling elites to achieve specific developmental goals and consensus (Deans, 2000). Historical specificities (path dependence), radical change in political institutions and external threats enable the governing elites to mobilise nationalism in economic policy. For example, in Taiwan and South Korea state elites were able to utilise the fear of take-over by their communist rivals to achieve this (Abbott, 2003). In the developmental state, the institutions have structured a weak link between state and societal groups relations, so the governing elite can easily use or manipulate nationalism in pursuit of industrial development. Ethno-economic development can also link to nationalist economic projects, especially in developing a country where the ethnic imperative is an important political consideration (Low, 2004; Case, 1994). Skilful political leaders can use symbols of nationalism or ethnic imperatives as an interpretative frame in industrial policy making with the intention to strategically intervene in the market (Abbott, 2004). This enables elites to mobilise resources with less chance of being challenged by specific organised groups.

The bureaucracy is one of the most important features in the developmental state approach. From neo-Weberian perspectives, Evans (1995) suggests that in a developmental state model, the bureaucracy plays an important role in constructing economic rules, implementing economic policies and exercising control to maintain the rules, ensuring the state's developmental outcome is attainable. The bureaucracy is filled with technocratic elites, staffed by the most able and highly qualified groups in the country. Furthermore, autonomous bureaucracy is central for the economic technocrats in a developmental state to form coherent economic policy (Wade, 1990).

Bureaucratic capacity and autonomy can provide the ability to devise long-term, coherent economic policies with less interference from private interest groups. Political insulation of the bureaucracy enables technocratic bureaucracy autonomy to shape development strategies and translate national goals into effective policy actions (Onis, 1991). This is parallel to Weberian bureaucracy, because ideally with bureaucratic insulations, the technocrats with specific expert knowledge are able to enforce rules and provide policy mechanisms to facilitate industrial development (Evans, 1995).

The close ties between state bureaucrats and 'selected' industrial groups enable the elite economic bureaucracy to create coherent development policies. This is what Evans (1995) terms as 'embedded autonomy' in a developmentalist state. 'Embedded autonomy' can be referred to as dense external ties between the elite economic bureaucrats and productive industrial groups in the society. Since the political institutions are able to insulate the state bureaucracy, the economic bureaucrats are able to independently formulate and implement policy while collaborate with the productive groups (Tan, 2009). The autonomous bureaucracy and the institutionalised close relationship between selected business elites and technocratic elites are able to form a dynamic export-oriented regime of industrial accumulations (Johnson, 1982). As industrial development requires close connections to private capital, such connections must be with 'selected' industrial groups, enabling state elites to incorporate these industrial groups into state economic projects. This embedded autonomy is also reflected in concrete social ties that enable state elites and industrial groups to continuously negotiate policy interests and resolve conflict, and eventually influences policy objectives.

State actors and 'selected enterprises' able to do this due to the institutional structures constrain the interactions of organised private interest groups that can potentially 'hijack' or undermine policy directions at state levels. Although developmentalist scholars have highlighted the crucial role of autonomous bureaucracy in industrial development, the degree of autonomy enjoyed by the bureaucracy in a developmental state is widely debated (Routely, 2012). Haggard (2004), Randall (2007), Moon and Prasad (1994), and Ramseyer and Rosenbluth (1993) argue that even though developmental states rely upon the 'rational' technocratic bureaucracy to plan and implement coherent economic policy, their actions remain influenced by political elites and industrial group interests because the mission and identified goals of bureaucrats are derived from the position of the governing elites (Onis, 1991). The broad policy interests still reflect upon the elite class' interests (Routely, 2012).

Variations of institutional design that adopt the developmental state approach may have different economic outcomes. Institutions that compose the organisation of the state are not homogenous (Weiss, 2000), and are a product of historical development, political process and normative regulations (Whitley, 1999). While a developmental state like Northeast Asia shows strong economic performance, different institutional environments may not necessarily be able to function similarly to the Northeast Asian developmental state style. Developing countries such as those in Southeast Asia (with the exemption of Singapore) that adopt a developmental state approach may not produce ‘stellar’ industrial growth like their counterparts. This is the reason why different institutions produce different developmental outcomes.

In developing countries, political institutions that are subject to wider social forces may undermine policy formations and implementation for industrial development. This links to state-society relations and the way that institutions structure distribution of power (Low, 2004). The ability of the state to manage development depends on the balance of political forces to shape the strength of the state in relation to society in contesting resources. As stated earlier, a developmental state’s power lies in its capacity to transfer resources to certain productive groups. Secondly, the state must be able to resolve conflict in transferring those resources between different segments of industrial groups, this includes overriding potential opposition groups that are left out in these transferring of resources (Tan, 2009, p. 155). However, in developing countries, established social classes, ethnic-based groups and an unproductive non-capitalist class exercise varying degree of political influence, which can compromise the state capacity to mobilise resources and direct economic outcome. The active social groups can undermine the transfer of resources, and some unproductive social groups can protect inefficient enterprises (Tan, 2008).

In a developmental state where state-business relations ingrained with political objectives can compromise industrial developmental outcome (Woo-Cumming, 1999). The interdependence of state and business is driven by short-term interest, as mainly political interests can be growth-reducing (Weiss & Hobson, 2000). Interdependence between state and business that has strong political consideration gives rise to the patron-client network. The patron-client network is a repeated relationship of exchange (usually through informal linkages) between patron and client. The nature of this relationship, institutionalised between state-society relationships, becomes a powerful interaction as it influences economic decisions (Gomez, 2002; Khan, 1998). The presence of strong patron influence in political institutions is unlikely to allow for planning or implementation of effective industrial policy. This is because political elites tend to extract resources to maintain clients (not based on economic consideration), and in this case resources are likely to be allocated to unproductive producers (Khan, 1998; Tan, 2008).

Patronage in developing countries becomes institutionally constrained because the distribution of state rents (subsidies, import licences or quota) is given to those who have close ties with the governing elites. Patron–client networks breed rent-seeking behaviour to secure economic rents. An economic rent ‘is a return to a resource owner in excess of the owner’s opportunity cost (Tollison, 1987, p. 144). Buchanan (1980) defines ‘rent-seeking as that part of the payment to an owner of resources that is over and above that which those resources could command in any alternative use’ (cited in Kang, 2002). Thus, rents are created when a political actor manipulates economic policy to distort prices and diverge from competitive levels. With the existence of rents, they are able to reap ‘excess profit’, because lucrative rent patronage is reinforced to gain access to the rents[1]. Corruption can occur when businessmen use bribery or other means in an attempt to influence policy decisions (Kang, 2002).

The problem with rent-seeking is that industrial policy can be captured by unproductive groups who have considerable political influence and personal connections, who organise resistance and develop ways to modify certain market outcomes politically (Alavi, 1982; Khan, 1998). Such groups continue to have access to state rent and can threaten any policy changes that undermine their interest. Furthermore, when an ethnic dimension is incorporated in the economic development due to post-colonial legacy, it marginalises certain groups. The ruling elites are perceived to only meet the material needs of certain ethnic groups in implementation of industrial policy (Jesudason, 1989). This strengthens rent-seeking behaviour and patronage between ruling elites with business groups fostered by political elites that depend on state rents under the auspice of ethnic development. Given the vested beholden interest between political and business elites, it can be difficult to transfer state rents to productive producers, which can compromise effective industrial policy implementation.

However, this does not suggest that the first tier developmental states of Northeast Asia are free from cronyism or the patron-client network, even though ethnic consideration is not their priority (given a homogenous society). Rather, the Japanese conglomerate *Keiretsus* or South Korea's *Chaebols* depends largely on state rents such as subsidies or other financial support to grow in the market. The state elites are in favour of large conglomerates to lead industrial development with a favourable investment climate, and the conglomerates are cronies of the state elites (Masina, 2002). The work of Kang (2002) and Khan (1998) reveals that patronage and money politics has been characterised as part of the industrial development of South Korea. The informal linkages between government and business exchange benefits through rent-seeking or patron-client networks, and policy interests are likely to favour certain groups of companies.

Even though patronage is part of the mode of exchange for benefits or altering policy terms (Kang, 2002), Weiss and Hobson (1995) point out that private enterprises mobilise and utilise resources for export-led growth. The existing state capacity enables the ruling elite to discipline private enterprise with market-based performance. Linkages are forged to ensure domestic companies are able to engage in industrial catch up with strong financial support from the government. The existing capacity enables the state to structure its market entry for certain foreign direct investments. Though rent-seeking may involve political and economic actors, Pempel (1999) argues that both are committed to high growth, realising that they would have to swim and sink together (p. 164). The patronage in Northeast Asia is used to promote growth-enhancing policy, while in some developing countries, when political gain subordinates economic objectives, patronage promotes growth-resisting policy (Low, 2004).

[1]For example, import licenses confer rents by restricting the volume of imported goods that come into a country, and thus those actors able to import the restricted goods will be able to sell those goods at a higher-than-market prices, thus obtaining rents (Kang, 2002, p. 180).

The state bureaucracy in most developing countries may not easily emulate the embedded autonomy seen in Northeast Asia. Embedded autonomy connects the state with productive social groups to form coordination in economic development but should not be captured (Evan, 1995). Once captured, it will lose its autonomy and become perverse and less *developmental*. This happens when political institutions prioritise political objectives over growth-enhancing policy, which leads to institutional constraints because elites transfer resources to accommodate certain groups that, though perhaps not productive, play an important political role in the society. Due to strong political consideration, the political elites will exert influence in the state bureaucracy to impose their interests that go beyond economic objectives. As such, the bureaucracy is no longer autonomous in economic planning and implementation of policy, because it is under the strong influence of the governing elites. Once captured by political elites and selected interest groups, state economic planning and configuration of interest reduce to private interest.

2.3 Political Economy of Malaysia's Policy-Making Process

The theoretical discussion in the previous section will be used to frame and analyse the political economy of Malaysia's policy-making institutions. The role of institutions, which this research leverages from historical and sociological perspectives, explains how institutions shape and facilitate the interaction of principle actors, and how they are subjected to wider institutional constraints based on political events, social context and historical specificities (Thelen, 1999; Steinmo, 2008). The power relations structured by the institutions affect interactions between actors. Furthermore, the normative dimension also influences how actors' behaviour operates in a particular institutional setting (Dimaggio, 1998; Scott, 2008). Hence, the role of institutions is to be the 'rules of the game' that constitute 'how things get done' in the policy-making process. Incorporating the developmental state approach explains how developing countries envision pursuit of long-term industrial development. The developmental state paradigm posits that the institutions of the state are structured by governing elite dominance, the role of bureaucracy and government-private relations (Moon & Prasad, 1994; Haggard, 1998; Onis, 1991). The institutional design enables a reciprocal relationship between government and private enterprise a way to design industrial policy to facilitate the growth of the domestic enterprises. The institutional arrangements underpin the role of political, bureaucracy elites and selected business groups to configure industrial policy preferences. The 'triangular arrangement' between these actors constitutes a vital policy community and their interactions have an impact on industrial policy.

In the context of Malaysia's policy-making institutions, when the country adopted a developmentalist state approach it underpinned the role of the political elites, bureaucrats and 'selected' business groups. In this research this is framed as a 'triangular arrangement'. These main actors are deemed as a policy community that can construct the 'rules of the games' (see Fig. 2.1). Institutional arrangements between

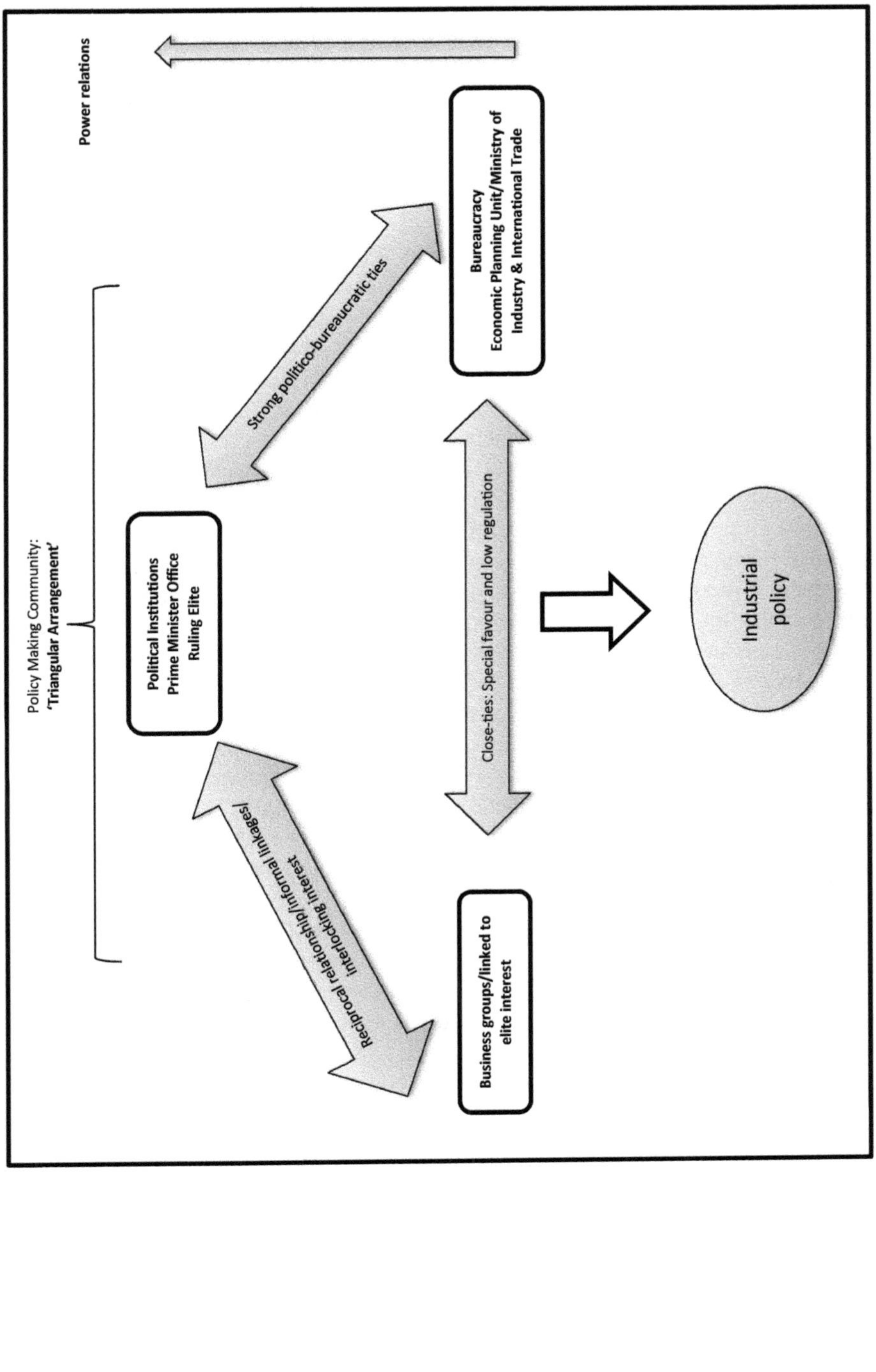

Fig. 2.1 Institutional arrangements for Malaysia policy making process

these agents are crucial to configure industrial policy. The institutional structure of Malaysia's economic policy making is best explained by the reference to the 'alignment' of the relationship between political, bureaucratic and business elites (Leigh, 1992). The direction of policy changes is interrelated with the three core actors' interactions.

Considering the historical specificities and social context in Malaysia, the power relations in the institutional arrangements lie in the political elites (executive branch) (further explanation below). That is, the existing structures enable the political elite to drive the policy development agenda. As a developmentalist state, 'the political elite are able to fend off distributional demands from other factions or individual within the ruling coalition, also to overcome resistance from societal groups to changes in institutions and rules which govern economic benefits' (Whitfield & Buur, 2014, p. 128). As such, the political elite can come out with industrial policy preferences and agenda. Having control of the political institutions and agenda setting, the political elite can transfer and allocate resources to drive certain segments of industry, under the rubric of national development (Doner, 1992). Pertinent to Malaysia's political institutions is the ethno-economic development of the Bumiputra group, which becomes a central part of political consideration in the industrial development project. The ruling coalition, which is led by UMNO and represents Bumiputra's interests, has dominant role to secure the ethno-economic requirement in policy-making institutions.

There is a close reciprocal relationship between the elites and selected business groups, such ties that exist during the formative years of industrialisation where this is an absence of industrialist groups. Most business groups are fostered by political elites who enable them to have access to state resources. The business groups can be labelled as a 'rentier class' (Searle, 1999; Gomez & Jomo, 1997; Tan, 2014) that has grown dependent upon rents generated by state elite. An important consideration in the context of Malaysia is that there are existing well-established industrial groups in the society. However, when ethnic consideration becomes part of developmental projects, the political elite by-pass the existing industrial groups and create new industrial groups that are ethnically determined (Jomo, 1990). The new business groups, in this case selected Bumiputra groups who are dependent on the state rents. The arm's length relationship between the ruling elite and business groups enables them to adjust policy terms in favour of the growth of groups. The ruling elite can divert resources to reduce risk for the group to invest in the market, even though in certain segments of the industry there is no comparative advantage. The state is able to facilitate through macroeconomic policy adjustment and allocate sufficient resources to grow with less opposition forces from other societal groups. This group relies on the ruling elite to obtain access to state resources, so power relations tend to lie with the political elite. Patronage then becomes the mode of exchange or interaction, due to interlocking interests between the political elite and the 'selected' business groups.

The dominant role of the political elite to formulate the industrial policy preferences agenda—is necessary but not sufficient. The political elite must have a significant degree of control over the state bureaucracy to exert interest in industrial policy implementation. In the case of Malaysia, the politico-bureaucratic relationship enables the elite to control the state institutions in the policy-making domain and direct economic outcomes (Searle, 1999). The role of the bureaucracy is to realise the policy interest of the elites and devise policy for the business groups to grow in the market. Here, the bureaucrats act as operating agents to the political elites and connect them to social groups (that may not be productive) whose function is to meet their interests. Certain predilections towards industrial policy are expected to ensure the groups' economic interest is likewise secured (Aun, 2004; Khalid & Mahani, 2014). Industrial policy being formulated tends to give certain privileges (implicit or explicit) to domestic enterprises such as low tax, de facto protective measures and financial supports or subsidies. Terms of policy are negotiable (either through formal or informal linkages) to facilitate the growth of the enterprises.

It is important to discuss the specific political institutions in Malaysia in order to further understand the political economy of policy-making institutions. The United Malay National Organisation (UMNO) is the main Malay political party that represents the interests of the largest community in Malaysia. UMNO has also built a political coalition as a means of power-sharing between the other main non-Malay political parties, including the Malaysian Chinese Association (MCA) and the Malaysia Indian Congress (MIC), as well as other minority political parties (Gomez, 2008). The ruling coalition is led by UMNO and has been the government for more than half of a century, since the formation of Malaysia in 1963. President of UMNO led BN will be the head (Prime Minister) of the executive government. Although, UMNO-led BN has been replaced by Pakatan Harapan after the 14th general election in 2018, the institutional legacy has retained the dominance role of the executive branch in deciding industrial policy preferences.

Malaysia's political institutions can be described as a consociational democracy, which refers to a government by elite cartel where political order might be maintained through power sharing so that the main ethnic communities are all represented in the government (Lijphart, 1977). In this sense, the consociationalist approach posits that there is somehow equal access for the elite from each ethnic group to compete for resources in the policy-making domain to reduce political tension (Means, 1991; Noh, 2013). Political fraction is reduced through this inter-elite bargaining and accommodation to foster inter-ethnic cooperation (Crouch, 1996). Inter-elite bargaining enables the political elite to set the rules of the game in their institutional structures, define how things are done and set a decision-making process based on formal and informal rules. This enables the country to meet the political and economic interests from each ethnic group to form a stable government (Leftwich, 2000).

Power sharing in the political coalition has changed after the racial riot in 1969. This episode changed the 'rules of the game' in the political institutions (Crouch, 1996). The riot happened due to the Chinese, who dominated the commercial and business activities, a fact that did not sit well with the majority Malays who were lagging behind in the mainstream of economic development. This created a critical juncture that changed the political inter-elite bargaining. The political institutions had structured the power relations to lie in the UMNO, which increased the Malay bargaining power to command economic resources (Noh, 2013; Mauzy, 1993). The ethnic disparities prompted the Malay political elites to correct economic imbalances with the formation of the New Economic Policy (NEP) [2]. The NEP is an affirmative action policy that institutionalised ethnic imperatives in socio-economic development policy. In the institutional context where 'race matters', the political elite (UMNO led coalition) may repress other ethnic groups' access to resources through what Mauzy (1993) terms as 'coercive consociationalist'. That is, the less dominant ethnic groups (for example the Chinese and Indian) tend to compromise with the more dominant ethnic group (Bumiputra) in the policy-making process.

When the state adopts a developmentalist state approach to pursue industrial development, executive branch in a political institution has the dominant role over the policy formulation. Policy ideas and problem recognition are confined to the executive branch, and though consultation takes place, discussion is limited to close allies to the Prime Minister (Leong, 1992; Gomez & Jomo, 1997; Lee, 2006; Aun, 2004; Chin, 2010). The parliament is supposed to be a check and balance for the policy arena, but it does little more than 'rubber-stamp' executive decisions (Brown et al., 2004; Khalid & Mahani, 2014). The longevity of the ruling coalition has rendered the executives with considerable power to impose their interests in the policy-making institutions.

Bureaucracies in a developmental state are important institutions to plan and implement economic policy. Technocratic elites play an important role in planning and enforcing economic policy. To this end, the political actors provide freedom for the technocrats to formulate and implement policy (Evan, 1995; Johnson, 1999). The space for the bureaucracy to act independently enables the bureaucrats to learn, get information from relevant R&D, formulate coherent economic policy and deploy effective coordination across the agencies to implement industrial policy at a target sector (Ritchie, 2009). However, bureaucracy captured by executive dominance enables the political elite to have dominant control over the state's institutions. Thus, the policy process tends to have a top-down approach, orchestrated by the political elite. Strong politico-bureaucratic nexus and institutional arrangements between them can influence the configuration of policy planning (Loh, 2015). Although the state bureaucracy operates based on the Weberian ideal, the task performed is based on codified rules (Lim, 2002). Through executive dominance, a political institution is able to intervene in bureaucratic institutions to exert their interest in the policy-making process (Chin, 2011). Bureaucratic institutions, captured by elites or their allies, enable them to secure compliance with the top government officials to realise policy interests despite possibly not being based on economic consideration (Menon, 2008). The politico-bureaucratic ties have rendered *layering* or *drifting* rules and policy to serve the interest of the governing elites (Siddeeque, 2006).

Strong politico-bureaucratic ties in Malaysia enable reciprocal relationships between political and bureaucratic elites. Particularly when the state begins to intervene in the marketplace to steer industrial development, the governing elites seek

[2]This affirmative action policy has been the guiding principle for distributive strategy for the subsequent government grand policy (Gomez, 2012, 2016) that is National Development Policy (NDP) (1990–2000), National Vision Policy (NVP) (2001–2010) and the recent New Economic Model (NEM) (2010–2020).

ways for the state institutions to realise elites' policy interests. Bureaucracy is an important source of power for governing elites to pursue interest in the policy domain (Ham & Hill, 1984 p. 53), and the dominant role of the political elites can exercise strong intervention in the bureaucracy to direct policy formation and implementation. The bureaucracy has considerable power in policy making because the state institution can mobilise revenue, come out with detailed planning, and implement funding and regulations, though policy interests largely come from the governing elites. Intervention from the political elites in policy implementation has somehow compromised the technocratic ability of the economic bureaucrats to carry out economic policy (Lim, 2002; Loh, 2015).

In Malaysia, policy-making institutions structure the Prime Minister's office and his department plays a central role in determining the broad direction of industrial policy. Following the developmental state approach, a key pilot agency to plan economic policy is essential to organize and direct industrial outcome. The Economic Planning Unit (EPU), part of the Prime Minister's department, is the primary site of the policy-making process. It has overarching influences over policy strategy and influences the allocation of resources. The unit is in charge of overseeing the development and implementation of medium and long-term economic strategies (Brown et al., 2004, p. 9). The EPU is one of the principle agencies in configuring economic policy, and it provides policy input to the highest level of decision-making of the country (Embong, 2012). The agency is staffed by technocrats who have specific expertise on economic policy. However, Henderson et al. (2002) point out that since the 1990s there has been a gradual demise of innovative-policy making at the EPU. The centralisation of economic policy making that revolves around the Prime Minister and private enterprises enables the elites to influence the state bureaucracy. Henderson et al. (2002) argue that the central site of economic policy formation, such as the EPU, has become an 'operation-oriented' body, rather than becoming technocrats to serve as an advising agency.

The Ministry of International Trade and Industry (MITI) is also one of the primary government bodies involved in policy formulation, inspired by the Japanese model. The key state bureaucracy, MITI plays a strategic role in planning and implementing policy. This ministry was established by Mahathir, then deputy Prime Minister, to oversee industrial development. This ministry, along with the EPU, coordinates industrial policy and makes necessary adjustments to the terms of policy to facilitate domestic enterprises. The MITI and EPU both hold formal policy discussions with various private sector and civil societies group with regards to annual budgets and other policy recommendations. This may present a formal open structure for other groups to provide policy input for the policy maker. However, Brown et al. (2004) observe that the formal policy dialogues may not achieve anything concrete because economic preferences and decision making is still largely centralised to the state elites (p. 8).

Policy interest of the industrial groups in the institutional arrangement can have impact on maintaining the status quo or bringing changes in industrial policy (Tham, 2015). They have the influence because the governing elites have interlocking interests with the business groups, since these groups are formed by the state elites and usually have close ties with the political elite. The close ties are further strengthened when the government under Mahathir's administration introduced its privatisation plan in the early 1990s, to transfer state-owned enterprises (SOE) to private ownership under the rubric of improving efficiency. The privatisation was a response to the SOEs crowding out the market during the NEP period. This led the government to privatise most SOEs. The privatisation plan was intended to create wealth for select individuals (not exclusively Bumiputra groups but other politically linked individuals as well) to run the formerly state-owned enterprises (Felker, 2003; Jomo, 1999). Thus, privatisation is not done in a transparent manner (Jomo & Wee, 2014), as the political elite handpicked rather than picking the winner to head private enterprise.

Patronage in appointment makes those who have close ties with the political elite the main beneficiaries in a privatisation plan. This forms a strong patronage between the business group and governing elites. The privatisation plan forms a high-level state-business network crucial in formulating policy. There is broad exercise of the patron-client network to enable business groups to have access to state resources through 'unusual' institutional arrangements (Tan, 2008). On another note, Jomo (1999, p. 5) and Gomez (2009, 2016) argue that the formation of the business group can become an important way to support and subsidise politically well-connected individuals. The existing institutional arrangement evolves around elites and with a strong patronage system, it is easily susceptible to regulator and political capture. Regulator captures are associated with favouring certain producers (even unproductive groups) over consumers. Political capture refers to when regulation becomes a tool for self-interest of the political elites (Tan, 2008). Consequences of regulatory and political captures lead to credible commitment problems in policy, misleading policy enforcement and biases in the mobilisation of resources.

Informal institutions can be powerful modes of exchange (Peng & Luo, 2000), given that existing institutional structures underpin informal rules to influence economic actors' interaction. As such, other private enterprises (not linked to state elites) or business associations will form informal institutional arrangements to exert their influences in the policy-making domain. Informal linkages include lobbying with principle economic actors to be exert their policy interest. Other economic actors may attempt to utilise the patron-client network to form institutional arrangements to advance or secure policy interests.

The role of international and regional institutions has implications on the institutional arrangements in Malaysia's policy-making institutions. Malaysia has to embrace some of the reforms required by the international or regional institutions in order to engage in global productions. Such as World Trade organisation (multilateral trading regimes), ASEAN (regionalist project) or ASEAN Free Trade Agreement (regional trade agreement)[3]. Whether it is multilateral (WTO) or regional trading

[3]The overarching objective of the World Trade Organisation (WTO) is to promote freer international trade regimes (Hoekman, 2002). There are a few basic principles that govern freer trade such as (i) non-discrimination, which has two features: most favoured nations (MFN) treating other people equally and national treatment treating foreign and locals equally; (ii) freer trade through negotiations; (iii) binding commitment and predictability; (iv) promoting fair competition; and (v) encouraging development and economic reform (see WTO). The WTO involves a complex

agreements (AFTA under ASEAN) both advocate trade liberalisation. The institutional arrangements involved with these institutions are market-based, whereby regulation is formed to reduce anticompetitive behaviour from trading partners (Freund & Ornelas, 2010; Baldwin, 1994). This is done to form a market-friendly environment, hence trade policy arrangements between members state are made to coordinate a freer trading regime. Trading partners have less barriers to enter the market and can expand market access without discrimination.

Malaysia's status as a member state to both the WTO and AFTA cannot ignore institutional arrangements coming from the international and regional trade agreement. Institutional arrangements from the agreements are made to expand market access for trading partners. Although wider market access could improve the overall economic welfare of the state, however policy actors are inevitably influenced by the domestic political economy demand (Tham, 2015). This is true especially when the presence of 'selected' domestic enterprises are framed as 'national interests' along with an ethnic imperative in which elite policy actors have substantial interests. Trade liberalisation is unlikely to occur straightforwardly because political actors will act according to what is appropriate based on the institutional context (Hall & Taylor, 1996). What is appropriate also depends on the elite policy actors' interpretations of the phenomenon (March & Olsen, 1989).

The multilateral and regional trade agreements will bring about pro-market reforms, where institutional arrangements are based on market relationships. This may limit the role of government in the marketplace. Having less control over the domestic economy (due to multilateral and regional agreements) may undermine the national interest and the growth of domestic enterprises in the marketplace. Hollingworth (2000) pointed out that the market relationship operates based on rules (with limited role of the state) to ensure that the market can operate at an optimum level. However, the institutional design underpins the role of the political elite, bureaucracy and 'selected' industrial groups in policy-making institutions. This provides the capacity to develop policy options to protect domestic enterprise interests. They are able to do so because the elite policy actors dominate policy institutions. There is limited access for other actors to influence policy for pro-market reforms.

The triangular relationship between these actors can structure market entry, as most developmentalist state approaches would structure a market-friendly environment while the state retains its strategic role facilitating the local private enterprises (Amsden, 2001; Whitley, 1999). Therefore, rules can be formulated to support a non-discriminatory environment, but at the same time the elite policy actors can come out

---

multilateral negotiation. Often it takes a longer period of time for member governments to agree on the binding commitment (Hoekman, 2002). On the other hand, regionalist projects like ASEAN give more flexibility for member states to negotiate regional trade agreements (RTA) like the ASEAN Free Trade Agreement (AFTA). RTA are an important trade policy tool to complement the multilateral trading system under the WTO (Fiorentino et al., 2007). This is the case so long as the RTA is consistent with the basic principles of the international trading system, specifically with non-discrimination. An RTA formed must minimise opportunistic behaviour that aims to discriminate against non-members (Hoekman & Schiff, 2002).

with institutional arrangements to favour the interest of the 'selected' domestic enterprises. Given that there is a strong reciprocal relationship between the government and domestic enterprises, institutional arrangements between them can craft policy space to protect the interest of the local private enterprises (Tham, 2004, 2015). It is expected that policy change will occur against the backdrop of trade liberalisation. The close links between elite policy actors can alter old rules to form new ones and re-interpret old rules within policy arrangements. Policy can be interpreted in a way that champions pro-market reforms, but institutional arrangements (formal or informal) between the elite policy actors and domestic enterprises can configure ways to craft policy space to coordinate the market to favour the 'selected' local enterprises. At the same time, they can devise select access to state resources to facilitate those enterprises to grow in the marketplace. Though multilateral and regional trade agreements are intended to create a freer trade regime and reduce market barriers, the state retains its strategic role to secure the 'selected' domestic enterprise, especially those enterprises linked to nationalist economic projects along with ethno-economic development (Doner, 1992).

2.4 Conclusion

To recapitulate, the aim of this research is to understand the political economy of industrial policy for a late industrialiser like Malaysia. While industrial policy has had significant impact on growth for developing countries over the past decades, this has prompted scholars to probe into the countries' institutional structures. This theoretical frame uses neo-institutionalism to understand how variations of institutional design can structure the organisation of political and economic actors and their relationships differently. The historical and social contexts of particular institutions influence the interaction of principle actors, which has implications in the policy-making process. The developmental state approach structures the strategic role of the state elites (politicians and bureaucrats) and selected business groups in policy making. Typical developmental state economic planning and coordination are orchestrated by the elites with less interference by organised groups. This gives advantage for the governing elites to mobilise, prioritise and coordinate policy preferences in the policy-making institutions. The governing elites have control over institutional arrangements to construct 'rules of the game', enabling elites to influence the policy-making institutions based on their interests, which can fall under the rubric of national development.

The discussion also explores institutional arrangements between economic actors, which elucidate how actors form institutional arrangements to reconcile and coordinate policy preferences. In a country that adopts a developmentalist state approach to development, the political and economic actors can form institutional arrangements to reconcile economic problems, promote interest and aggregate preferences to take place beyond arm's length relationships. The reciprocal relationship between state elites and domestic enterprise linked to the elites enables elites to configure policy accommodating the interest of their business allies in the market. The structures of power relations in the institutional arrangement also influence the coordination of economic preferences. In each mode of institutional arrangement, it can be argued that the continuum of power relations lies within the state elites.

In the context of Malaysia's policy-making institutions, the tripartite arrangement between political elites, bureaucrats and domestic industrial groups (who are linked to state elites) can determine policy choices. The governing elites can come out with developmental goals and they have the power to adjust and refine policy formulation. The elites can also provide preferential access to state rent for industrial groups. Institutional arrangements form these actors is crucial in configuring and interpreting policy preferences.

References

Abbott, J. (2003). *Developmentalism and dependency in Southeast Asia*. London: Routledge.

Abbott, J. (2004). 'Not like the rest': Differential development in Malaysia and Thailand. In L. Low (Ed.), *Developmental state: Relevancy, redundancy or reconfiguration?* New York: Nova Science Publisher.

Alavi, H. (1982). State and class under peripheral capitalism. In H. Alavi & T. Shanin (Eds.), *Introduction to the sociology of developing countries*. London: Macmillan Press.

Amsden, A. H. (2001). *The rise of 'the rest': Challenges to the west from late industrialising economies*. Oxford University Press.

Aun, L. H. (2004). Development in Malaysia: Economics and politics of idea. *Akademia, 64*, 65–81.

Baldwin, R. (1994). *Towards an integrated Europe* (p. 2). Chapter: CEPR.

Beissinger, M. R., & Young, C. (2002) Introduction: Comparing state crises across two continents. In M. Beissinger & C. Young (Eds.), *Beyond state crisis? Post-colonial Africa and post-Soviet Eurasia in comparative perspective*. Washington, DC.

Boettke, P. J., Coyne, C. J., & Leeson, P. T. (2008). Institutional stickiness and the new development economics. *American Journal of Economics and Sociology, 67*(2).

Braathen, E. (1996). New institutionalism in development studies: Weberian contributions. *Forum for Development Studies, 23*(2), 215–241.

Brown, G. K., Ali, S. H., & Muda, W. M. W. (2004). *Policy lever in Malayia*. Centre for Research on Inequality, Human Security and Ethnicity (CRISE), University of Oxford, Queen Elizabeth House.

Buchanan, J. (1980). Rent seeking and profit seeking. In J. M. Buchanan, R. D. Tollison, & G. Tullock (Eds.), *Toward a theory of the rent-seeking society*. College Station: Texas A and M University Press.

Campbell, J. L. (1997). Recent trends in institutional political economy. *The International Journal of Sociology and Social Policy, 17*(7/8), 15–56.

Campbell, J. L. (1998). Institutional analysis and the role of ideas in political economy. *Theory and Society, 27*(3), 377–409.

Campbell, J. L., & Pedersen, O. K. (2001). Introduction: The rise of neoliberalisation and institutional analysis. In J. L. Campbell & O. K. Pedersen (Eds.), *The rise of neoliberalisation and institutional analysis* (pp. 1–24). New Jersey, Oxfordshire: Princeton University Press.

Case, W. (1994). Elites and regimes in comparative perspective: Indonesia, Thailand, and Malaysia. *Governance: An International Journal of Policy and Administration, 7*(4), 431–460.

Castell, M. (1992). Four Asian tigers with a dragon head: A comparative analysis of the state, economy, and society in the Asian Pacific Rim. In R. Applebaum & J. Henderson (Eds.), *States and development in the Asian Pacific Rim*. London: Sage.

Chin, J. (2010). A decade later: The lasting Shadow of Mahathir. In J. Chin & J. Dosch. *Malaysia post-Mahathir: A decade of change*. Singapore: Marshall Cavendish International (Asia).

Chin, J. (2011). Future of democracy in Malaysia. *Panoroma: Insights into Asian and European Affairs, 2*(10), 81–91.

Collin, K. (2002). Clans, pacts, and regime transitions in Central Asia. *Conference on Informal Institutions and Politics in the Developing World*, Weatherhead Center for International Affairs, Harvard University.

Crouch, H. (1996). *Government and society in Malaysia*. Ithaca, NY: Cornell University Press.

Deans, P. (2000). The capitalist development in East Asia. In R. P. Palan & J. P. Abbott (Eds.), *State strategies in the global political economy*. London: Pinter.

DiMaggio, P. J. (1998). The new institutionalisms: Avenues of collaboration. *Journal of Institutional and Theoretical Economics, 154*(4), 696–705.

DiMaggio, P. J., & Powell, W. W. (1983). The iron cage revisited: Institutional isomorphism and collective rationality in organizational fields. *American Sociological Review, 48*(2), 147–160.

DiMaggio, P. J., & Powell, W. W. (Eds.). (1991). *The new institutionalism in organizational analysis*. Chicago: University of Chicago Press.

Dobbin, F. (2004). The sociological view of the economy. In F. Dobbin (Ed.), *The new economic sociology: A reader* (pp. 1–48). Princeton and Oxford: Princeton University Press.

Doner, R. F. (1992). Limits of state strength: Toward an institutionalist view of economic development. *World Politics, 44*(3), 398–431.

Embong, A. R. (2012). Developmental state capacity and institutional reforms. In B. T. Khoo (Eds.), *Policy regimes and political economy of poverty reduction in Malaysia*. United Nations Research Institute for Social Development UNRISD.

Evans, P. (1995). *Embedded autonomy, states and industrial transformation*. Princeton: Princeton University Press.

Felker, G. (2003). Mahathir and politics of economic policy making in Malaysia. In B. Welsh (Ed.), *Reflections: The Mahathir Years*. Johns Hopkins U. School of Advanced International Studies.

Fiorentino, R. V., Verdeja, L., & Toqueboeuf, C. (2007). *The changing landscape of regional trade agreements: 2006 update* (The WTO Discussion Paper No. 12). Geneva: The World Trade Organization.

Freund, C., & Ornelas, E. (2010). Regional trade agreements: Blessing or burden? *CEPR Portal*. https://voxeu.org/article/regional-trade-agreements-blessing-or-burden.

Gomez, E. T. (2002). *Political business in East Asia*. London: Routledge.

Gomez, E. T. (2008). Enterprise development and inter-ethnic relations in Malaysia: affirmative action, generational change, and business partnerships. In S. K. W. Raymon. *Chinese entrepreneurship in a global era*. London: Routledge.

Gomez, E. T. (2009). The rise and fall of capital: Corporate Malaysia in historical perspectives. *Journal of Contemporary Asia, 39*(3), 345–381.

Gomez, E. T. (2016). Resisting the fall: The single dominant party, policies and elections in Malaysia. *Journal of Contemporary Asia*.

Gomez, T. (2012). The politics and policies of corporate development: Race, rent and redistribution in Malaysia. In H. Hill, S. Y. Tham, & M. Z. Ragayah (Eds.), *Malaysia development challenges: Graduating from the middle*. New York: Routledge.

Gomez, E. T., & Jomo, K. S. (1997). *Malaysia's political economy: Politics, patronage and profits*. Cambridge: Cambridge University Press.

Gourevitch, P. (1986). *Politics in hard times*. Ithaca: Cornell University Press.

Haggard, S. (1998). Business, politics and policy in East and Southeast Asia. In S. R. Henry (Ed.), *Behind East Asia growth: The political and social foundations of prosperity*. London: Routledge.

Haggard, S. (2004). Institutions and growth in East Asia. *Comparative International Development, 38*(4), 53–81.

Hall, P. A. (1986). *Governing the economy: The politics of state intervention in Britain and France*. New York: Oxford University Press.

Hall, P. A. (1997). The role of interests, institutions, and ideas in the comparative political economy of the industrialized nations. In M. I. Lichbach & A. S. Zuckerman (Eds.), *Comparative politics: Rationality, culture, and structure*. Cambridge: Cambridge University Press.

Hall, P. A., & Taylor, R. C. R. (1996). Political science and the three new institutionalisms. *Political Studies, 44*(5), 936–957.

Hall, P. A. A. D. S. (Ed.). (2001). *Varieties of capitalism: the institutional foundations of comparative advantage*. Oxford: Oxford University Press.

Ham, C., & Hill, M. (1984). *The policy process in the modern capitalist state*. UK: The Harvester Press Publication Group.

Helmke, G., & Levitsky, S. (2004). Informal institutions and comparative politics: A research agenda. *Perspective on Politics, 2*(4), 725–740.

Henderson, J. (1993). The role of the state in the economic transformation of East Asia. In C. Dixon & D. Drakakis-Smith (Eds.), *Economic and social development in Pacific Asia*. London: Routledge.

Henderson, J., Hulme, D., Philips, R., & Nur, N. A. (2002). Economic governance and poverty reduction in Malaysia, Globalisation and Poverty.

Hodgson, G. M. (1999). *Economics and utopia*. London: Routledge.

Hoekman, B. (2002). The WTO: functions and basic principles. In B. Hoekman, A. Mattoo, & P. English (Eds.), *Development, trade and the WTO: A handbook*.

Hoekman, B., & Schiff, M. (2002). Benefitting from regional integration. In B. Hoekman, A. Mattoo, & P. English (Eds.), *Development, trade and the WTO: A handbook*.

Hollingworth, R. J. (2000). Doing institutional analysis: Implication for the study of innovation. *Review of International Political Economy, 7*(4), 595–644.

Jenniver, S. (2009). *The politics of water institutional reforms in neopatrimonial state*. Springer.

Jesudason, J. V. (1989). *Ethnicity and the economy: State, Chinese business and multinational in Malaysia*. Singapore: Oxford University Press.

Johnson, C. (1982). *MITI and the Japanese miracle: The growth of industrial policy, 1925–75*. Stanford University Press.

Johnson, C. (1999). The developmental state: Odyssey of a concept. In M. Woo-Cumings (Ed.), *The developmental state*. Ithaca: Cornell University Press.

Jomo, K. S. (1990). Whither Malaysia new economic policy? *Pacific Affairs, 63*(4), 469–499.

Jomo, K. S. (1999). Development planning in Malaysia: A critical appraisal. In B. N. Ghosh & M. S. Salleh (Eds.), *Political economy of development in Malaysia*. Malaysia: Utusan Publication and Distribution Sdn Bhd.

Jomo, K.S. (2004) Southeast Asian developmental state in comparative East Asian perspectives, in Linda, L. (ed) *Developmental state: Relevancy, redundancy or reconfiguration?* Nova Publishers.

Jomo, K. S., & Wee, C. H. (2014). *Malaysia@50: Economic development, distribution and disparities*. Strategic Information and Research Development Malaysia.

Kang, D. C. (2002). Bad loans to good friends: Money politics and the developmental state in South Korea. *International Organization, 56*(1), 177–207.

Khan, M. (1998). Patron-client networks and the economic effects of corruption in Asia. *European Journal of Development Research, 10*(1), 15–39.

Khalid, M. K., & Mahani, Z. A. (2014). Technocracy in economic policy-making in Malaysia. *Southeast Asian Studies, 3*(2), 383–413.

Koo, H., & Kim, E. M. (1992). The developmental state and capital accumulation in South Korea. In R. Applebaum & J. Henderson (Eds.), *States and development in the Asian Pacific Rim*. London: Sage.

Krasner, S. D. (1988). Sovereignty: An institutional perspective. *Comparative Political Studies, 21*(1), 66–94.

Lauridsen, L. S. (1995). The developmental state and the Asian Miracle: An introduction to the debate. *International Development Studies*. Roskilde Universitet.

Lee, S. J. (2006). The demise of Korea, Inc.: Paradigm shift in Korea's developmental state. *Journal of Contemporary Asia, 36*(3): 305–24.
Leftwich, A. (2000). *States of development: On the primacy of politics in development*. Cambridge: Polity Press.
Leftwich, A. (2010). Beyond institutions: Rethinking the role of leaders, elites and coalitions in the institutional formation of developmental states and strategies. *Forum for Development Studies, 37*(1), 93–111.
Leigh, M. (1992). Politics, bureaucracy and business in Malaysia: Realigning the eternal triangle. In M. Andrew & J. Kanishka (Eds.), *The dynamics of economic policy reforms in Southeast Asia and the Southwest Pacific*. Singapore: Oxford University Press.
Leong, H. K. (1992). Dynamic of policy making in Malaysia: The formulation of the new economic policy and the national development policy. *Asian Journal of Public Administration, 14*(2).
Lewellen, T. C. (2003). *Political anthropology: An introduction*. London.
Lijphart, A. (1977). *Democracy in plural societies*. London: Yale University Press.
Lim, H. H. (2002). Public administration: the effect of the executive dominance. In K. W. Loh & T. B. Khoo (Eds.), *Democracy in Malaysia: Practices and discourse*. Nordic Institute of Asian.
Loh, K. W. (2015). Centralised federalism in Malaysia: is change in the offing? In W. Bridget & W. Meredith (Eds.), *Routledge handbook of Contemporary Malaysia*. Routledge.
Low, L. (2001). The Singapore developmental state in the new economy and polity. *The Pacific Review, 14*(3), 411–441.
Low, L. (2004). *Developmental state: Relevancy, redundancy or reconfiguration?* Nova Publishers.
Mahoney, J., & Thelen, K. (2010). A theory of gradual institutional change. In M. James & T. Kathleen (Eds.), *Explaining institutional change: Ambiguity, agency, and power*. New York: Cambridge University Press.
March, J. G., & Olsen, J. P. (1984). The new institutionalism: Organisational factors in political life. *American Political Science, 78*(3), 734–749.
March, J. G., & Olsen, J. P. (1989). *Rediscovering institutions*. New York: Free Press.
Masina, P. (2002). *Rethinking development in East Asia: From illusory miracle to economic crisis*. Routledge Curzon.
Mason, J. (1996). *Qualitative researching*. London, UK: Sage.
Mauzy, D. K. (1993). Malaysia: Malay political hegemony and "coercive consociationalism. In J Ma B O Leary (Ed.), *The Politics of ethnic conflict regulation: case studies of protracted ethnic conflicts*. Oxford: Routledge.
Means, G.P. (1991). *Malaysian Politics: The second generation*. Oxford University Press.
Menon, J. (2008). *Macroeconomic management amid ethnic diversity: Fifty years of Malaysian experience* (ADB Institute Discussion Paper No. 102).
Meyer, J. W. (2010). World society, institutional theories, and the actor. *Annual Review of Sociology, 36*, 1–20.
Moon, C. I., & Prasad, R. (1994). Beyond the developmental state: Network, politics and institutions. *Governance: An International Journal of Policy, Administration and Institutions, 7*(4), 360–386.
Noh, A. (2013). *Malaysia and the consociational option: Is there a path dependent logic*. Abdul Razak School of Government (Working Paper 2013/01).
North, D. (1991). Institutions. *The Journal of Economic Perspectives, 5*(1), 97–112.
O'Donnell, G. (1996). *Another institutionalisation: Latin America and elsewhere* (Kellogg Institute Working Paper 222).
Onis, Z. (1991). The logic of the developmental state. *Comparative Politics, 24*(1), 109–126.
Pempel, T. J. (1999). The development regime in a changing world economy. In M. Woo-Cummings (Ed.), *The developmental state*. London: Cornell University Press.
Peng, M. W., & Luo, Y. (2000). Managerial ties and firm performance in a transition economy: The nature of a micro-macro link. *Academy of Management Journal, 43*(3), 486–501.
Ramseyer, J. M., & Rosenbluth, F. M. (1993). *Japan's political market place*. Cambridge, MA: Harvard University Press.

Randall, V. (2007). Political parties and democratic developmental states. *Development Policy Review, 25*(5), 633–652.

Ritchie, B. K. (2009). Economic upgrading in a state-coordinated, liberal market economy. *Asia Pacific Journal of Management, 26,* 435–457.

Routely, L. (2012). *Developmental state: A review of the literature* (Effective States and Inclusive Development (ESiD) Working Paper No. 03).

Schattschneider, E. E. (1957). Intensity, visibility, direction and scope. *The American Political Science Review, 51*(4), 933–942.

Scott, W. R. (2001). *Institutions and organizations* (2nd ed.). Thousand Oaks: Sage.

Scott, W. R. (2008). *Institutions and organizations: Ideas and interests.* Los Angeles: Sage Publications.

Searle, P. (1999). *The riddle of Malaysia capitalism.* Allen and Unwin: Australia.

Sewell, W. H. (1996). *Three temporalities: Toward an eventful sociology.* Ann Arbor: University of Michigan Press.

Siddeeque, N. A. (2006). Paradoxes of public accountability in Malaysia: Control mechanism and their limitations. *International Public Management Review, 7*(2), 43–65.

Steinmo, S. (1993). *Taxation and democracy: Swedish, British and American approaches to financing the modern state.* New Haven: Yale University Press.

Steinmo, S. (2008). Historical institutionalism. In D. D.Porta & M. Keating (Eds.), *Approaches and methodologies in the social science: A pluralist perspectives.* Cambridge University Press.

Tan, J. (2009). Can the East Asian developmental state be replicated? The case of Malaysia. In R. Springborg (Ed.), *Development models in Muslim context.* Edinburgh University Press.

Tan, J. (2008). *Privatisation in Malaysia: Regulation, rent-seeking and policy failure.* Routledge.

Tan, J. (2014). Running out of steam? Manufacturing in Malaysia. *Cambridge Journal of Economics, 38,* 153–180.

Tham, S. Y. (2004). The future of industrialisation in Malaysia under WTO. *Asia pacific Development Journal, 11*(1).

Tham, S. Y. (2015). Trade liberalization and national autonomy: Malaysia's experience at the multilateral and bilateral Levels. In J. M. Nelson, J. Meerman, & A. R. Embong (Eds.), *Globalisation and national autonomy: The experience of Malaysia.* Singapore: Institute of Southeast Asian Studies (ISEAS).

Thelen, K. (1999). Historical institutionalism in comparative politics. *Annual Review of Political Science, 2*(1), 369–404.

Thelen, K. (Ed.) (2002). *The explanatory power of historical institutionalism.* Frankfurt.

Thelen, K., & Steinmo, S. (1992). Historical institutionalism in comparative politics. In S. Steinmo, K. Thelen, & F. Longstreth (Eds.), *Structuring politics: Historical institutionalism in comparative analysis* (pp. 1–32). Cambridge, Melbourne: Cambridge University Press.

Tollison, R. D. (1987). Is the theory of rent-seeking here to stay? In C. K. Rowley (Ed.), *Democracy and public choice.* Oxford: Basil Blackwell.

Wade, R. (1990). *Governing the market: Economic theory and the role of government in East Asian industrialization.* Princeton, NJ: Princeton University Press.

Weiss, L. (2000). Developmental states in transition: adapting, dismantling, innovating, not 'normalizing'. *The Pacific Review, 12,* 21–55.

Weiss, L., & Hobson, J. M. (1995). *States and economic development: A comparative historical analysis.* Cambridge: Polity Press.

Weiss, L., & Hobson, J. M. (2000). *States and economic development: A comparative historical analysis.* Cambridge: Polity Press.

Whitfield, L., & Buur, L. (2014). The politics of industrial policy: ruling elites and their alliances. *Third Quarterly, 35*(1), 126–144.

Whitley, R. (1999). *Divergent capitalisms: The social structuring and change of business systems.* Oxford: Oxford University Press.

Woo-Cumming, M. (1999). Introduction: Chalmers Johnson and the politics of nationalism and development. In M. Woo-Cumings (Ed.), *The developmental state.* Ithaca, NY: Cornell University.

Chapter 3
Malaysia Automotive Policy and Industrial Policy

3.1 Industrial Nationalism: The Heavy Industrialisation Programme and Birth of National Car Projects

Under the tenure of Prime Minister Mahathir Mohammad, aggressive industrial policy is spelled out as part of the government's strategy to modernise the economy through industrialisation (Menon, 2008). Mahathir's leadership is a turning point for Malaysia's economic orientation and industrial policy strategy. The government strategy during the 1980s also attempted to address the problem associated with the strategy of local content during the early period of promoting the automotive industry. The localisation policy has a limited spinoff effect for the domestic automotive industry because domestic manufacturers are restricted to small medium enterprises in mid or low tier functions, such as assembly and subcontracting. Linkages built on the foreign automakers are limited, thus leading to a weak technological base and very shallow industrial specialisation (Embong, 1996; Menon, 2008; Tan, 2014; Kanapthy, 2001).

To address this problem, the government launched the heavy industrialisation programme. The plan of heavy industrialisation is in line with the 'Look East Policy',[1] an industrialisation strategy that emphasises the role of the state to facilitate domestic firms in industrial deepening and upgrading, including in Northeast Asian countries such as Japan and South Korea (Lall, 2000; Jomo & Wee, 2014). Unlike Northeast Asia's (particularly South Korea and Japan) automotive industry that benefited industrially during the Japanese occupation, Malaysia does not have a strong industrial base for the automotive industry (Abdulsomad, 1999; Machado, 1994). The heavy industrialisation plan requires a 'big push' from the state because it needs

[1] In this policy, announced by Prime Minister Mahathir Mohammad, the industrial development strategy is modelled along Northeast Asia's (Japan, South Korea and Taiwan) industrialisation strategy. The Northeast Asian governments employed the developmentalist state approach, 'where the government provides protection, credit allocation and subsidies, FDI restrictions, and skills and technology support to induce domestic firms to enter difficult activities, raise local content and take on advanced technological functions' (Lall, 2000, p. 6).

F. Suffian, *Political Economy of Malaysia's Industrial Policy*,
https://doi.org/10.1007/978-981-33-6901-6_3

a substantial amount of investment to embark on the program at the outset. There is a need for the state to facilitate building the industrial development capacity (Embong, 1996). Direct state involvement is necessary to facilitate the automotive industry because private firms lack initial capital to venture into heavy industrial development. The state acts as an entrepreneur to start up the considerable amount of capital investments to facilitate the growth of heavy industry (Kanapthy, 2001). The heavy Industrialisation programme has shifted the state resources, which initially Malaysia had limited comparative advantage (Mehmet, 1999). Shortly after the announcement of the heavy industrialisation plan, the government came out with its first Industrial Master Plan (IMP 1986–1995), which envisaged that the automotive industry would lead in self-development mode with the formation of the national car project (Tai & Ku, 2013; Doner, 1992; Abdulsomad, 1999).

The state involvement in the heavy industrialisation program is also seen as way to attain ethnic redistribution and to reduce economic inequality across races (Jomo, 1993; Gomez & Jomo, 1997; Embong, 1996, 2012; Tan, 2008). The automotive industry is deemed to be one of the strategic industries that involves various production processes and specialisation that the state can link to the domestic firms in the industry with protectionist measures. The heavy industrialisation plan through the national car project can increase participation of the Bumiputra community in the auto industry at different levels of production. Furthermore, there are additional spin-offs for the community to seize such as managerial positions, engineers and technical experts. Basically, the long-term plan is to foster Bumiputra not just to be ordinary assemblers but as engineers that can design their own vehicle. By emphasising the focus on Bumiputra to be incorporated in the automobile business, it is an attempt by the state to 'bypass' those competent existing vendors (mainly Chinese) (Jomo, 2007).

Mahathir set up the Heavy Industries Corporation Malaysia (HICOM), a state-owned enterprise (later privatised in 1990s) that focuses on developing main industries such as petrochemical, iron and steel, cement, paper products, machinery, and transport equipment (Tan, 2014). The main objective of HICOM is to lead the heavy industrialisation programme by building and strengthening the foundation of manufacturing sectors by providing forward and backward linkages for the development of heavy industries (Menon, 2008). This is also to enable the transfer of knowledge to domestic enterprises in order to be competent in industrial activities. The government fashioned the programme with economic nationalism, in which the domestic firms (particularly led by Bumiputra groups) should lead industrial development with less dependence on foreign companies (Embong, 1996). The heavy industrialisation project resulted in high import quota, import duties and excise duties to protect the growth of strategic industries, including the automotive industry. This project also emphasises the interest to create wealth among selected groups in the society, particularly Bumiputra industrialist groups (Tan, 2014).

In 1983 Perusahan Otomobile Sendirian Berhad, or simply Proton, was launched as the first national car project. The establishment of the national car project was a joint venture between HICOM and the Mitsubishi Motor Corporation (Rosli, 2006). HICOM held 70% of the share in the company and Mitsubishi Motor Corporation

(MMC) had the remaining 30% (Jomo, 1994). HICOM became the main shareholder through a RM33 million loan arranged by Mitsubishi. Jayasankaran (1994) observes that the deal with MMC led by Mahathir was done in almost total secrecy and there is dearth of information about the project available to the public. The national car project was also carried out without the cabinet approval at the outset. Furthermore, Mahathir did not make any attempt to open the options to other foreign firms for competitive bidding. By all accounts, the Prime Minister believed that MMC was the best Japanese automaker in the aspect of building national ambition.

The objective of producing the national car was mainly for the domestic market at the outset (later for export). This is in contrast to neighbouring countries, particularly Thailand, where the strategy is opening up for Foreign Direct investment (FDIs) and Join Venture (JV) in order to be integrated in the global vehicle production network (Tham, 2003; Natsuda & Thoburn, 2014). By pursuing the national car project, the government envisaged the ability to rationalise the automobile industry, promote related industry, enhance utilisation of locally-made components, encourage upgrading of technology, and improve economics of scale among local manufacturers that link to the national car production chain. Above all, the national car project required over 20,000 components and this could increase Bumiputra involvement as suppliers in the industry (Jomo, 2007; Anazawa, 1997, 2006; Torri, 1991). In 1983, the first Proton plant was built in the HICOM industrial estate and was designed to produce 80,000 car units. Its capacity was extended to 120,000 units in 1988. In 1985, Proton began with its first inaugural model, the Saga (1300cc and 1500cc engines), which was based on the Mitsubishi Lancer Model.

A few years after the launch of the national car, Malaysia suffered from the world economic crisis at the end of 1986. The world commodity slump was one of the worst crises the country suffered since the formation of Malaysia in 1963. The automobile industry was one of the sectors that was badly affected by the economic recessions. The economy became weak due to the balance of payment deficit caused by a massive depreciation of the Malaysian currency. This was compounded by a sharp increase of the yen after the Plaza Accord in 1985, which eventually led Proton to the huge burden of repaying the start-up loan in yen (Abdulsomad, 1999). Furthermore, to buy CKDs kits and auto parts from Japan, the steep appreciation of the yen increased Proton's cost of production. As a result, Proton recorded continuing losses from 1985 until 1988. However, it did not take long for the national car to bounce back in the market. After the recovery in 1989, Proton became a popular car in Malaysia and by 1995 the national car managed to capture 78.7% of the domestic passenger car market and started exporting to 28 countries (Hasan & Jomo, 2007).

The agreement between Proton and Mitsubishi left a grey area relating to export for Proton cars (Machado, 1994). It was clear in the agreement that for five years Mitsubishi would help produce a car for the domestic market. The time for Proton to dominate the domestic market was faster than expected because of the tariffs imposed on other foreign automakers. After the commodity slumps in the late 1980s, the government realised that relying on the domestic market was not enough for Proton to increase sales. The export of the national car seemed pertinent in order to sustain Proton production and attain economies of scales (Jomo, 1994). However, Mitsubishi resisted facilitating the Proton as an export because it would directly compete with Mitsubishi cars between the range of 1.3cc and 1.6cc produced in Japan and Thailand. Also, Mitsubishi felt reluctant because the Saga model had lower quality, being like a downgraded version of the Mitsubishi Lancer (Bartu, 1992).

However, after the economic crisis, Proton started to export abroad and made arrangements for marketing independently from Mitsubishi under the directive of Mahathir Mohammad (Jomo, 1993). The national carmaker signed an agreement with Mainland Investment, a car dealer in the UK, for the low-end car market in the country (Athukorala, 2014). Proton managed to compete with Lada from the Soviet Union and Zastava from Yugoslavia in this category in the UK. At that time, the Saga model had a price advantage because it qualified for free import duty to the UK under the Generalised Scheme of Preferences. By the 1990s, Proton managed to export over 10,000 units, but the national carmaker was unable to sustain in the long term, due to stiff competition from other Japanese and Korean cars with better images and quality (Jomo, 1994). In 1986, Proton intended to work with Bricklin Industries Inc. of New York, a car distributor in the US that had successfully imported a Yugoslavian car, the Yugo, to the US market. Working with Bricklin would give Proton a new milestone by gaining access to the lucrative US market. Although the US company intended to sell 100,000 units for Proton, the company failed to obtain technical approval from US authorities for the import of the Proton Saga model.

As an attempt to diversify the automotive industry, in 1991 Prime Minister Mahathir announced the second national car project, Perusahana Otomobile Kedua, also known as Perodua. The project mainly focused on small cars that were not direct competition for Proton models. Basically, the second national car project began in order to create a new lower middle-class car market (Athukorala, 2014; Wad, 2009; Wad & Govindaraju, 2011). Perodua was established as a joint venture with Daihatsu Motor (associated with Toyota), and started its production of the 660cc capacity Kancil model (based on Daihatsu Mira). Like Proton, the second national car project received similar tariff concessions and other government supports. Perodua is considered as a national car despite the fact that the manufacturing subsidiaries are 51% equity controlled by Daihatsu Motor Co. and Mitsui & Co., and in effect the Japanese Daihatsu holds the majority share in the second 'national' car project (Rosli, 2006; Wad & Govindaraju, 2011). In 1995, the government introduced Modenas, a local motorcycle manufacturing joint venture with Japan's Kawasaki. In the same year, the government also established the Malaysia Truck and Bus company (MTB) with Japan's Isuzu, which focused on commercial vehicles. In 1997, INOKOM was set up to produce light commercial vehicles with joint investment by Sime Darby Malaysia and Hyundai Motor Company (Doner & Wad, 2014). With the introduction of several national car projects, they were expected to utilise the Proton vendor network and other local firms.

The government became increasingly concerned with the partnership between Proton and Mitsubishi. The purpose of forging partnership with the Japanese company was to build Proton as an internationally competitive, self-sufficient car, not simply a vehicle stamped by Mitsubishi that continued to use their parts and components (Natsuda et al., 2013). The partnership did not achieve this end, as

Mitsubishi resisted transferring technology and exporting the national car (Jomo, 1994; Athukorala, 2014). There was no clear technology transfer to the Proton because Mitsubishi also resisted using local vendors as parts and components suppliers. In practice, Proton just assembled the auto parts imported from Japan. Furthermore, Mitsubishi tended to provide outdated technology with high management fees and cost of auto parts imported from the Mitsubishi production network (Jomo, 1993; Machado, 1994). The intention of the joint venture was to build Proton as competitive vehicles for export. Focusing on the domestic market itself was not sufficient for the national car company to achieve economic of scales due to the small market, hence export was necessary.

By 2004, Mitsubishi was trying to sell its shares because the company suffered from bad sales performance in North America. At the same time, the national car company already acquired 64% of the equity in Lotus Group International Ltd, a British automotive company. Later, in 2003, Proton became the main shareholder of Lotus Group. Mitsubishi sold its stake to Khazanah National, a government investment arm, and to Petronas, the national oil company (in 2012 they sold them back to DRB-HICOM). This earmarked Mitsubishi's exit from the national car company and allowed Proton to become a fully Malaysian-owned company.

3.2 Protectionist Policy for National Carmakers

There was strong support and protective measures from tariff and non-tariff barriers to other direct and indirect financial supports from the state to the national carmakers, especially during the early stage. The protective measure is to improve production, address the lack of skills and expand the domestic market (Rosli, 2006). In the 1980s and late 1990s, the government set a heavy tariff for automobile sectors. The Malaysian government imposed a tariff on CBUs passenger vehicles between 90 and 200% in 1982. In 1997, the Malaysian import tariff rose between 140 and 300% of the import tariff for CBUs car, particularly for foreign cars with engine capacities within the range of 1200cc and 1600cc. The import tariffs imposed by the government were higher than those in Thailand, which levied an 80% tariff for CBUs in the same year. Thailand, after changing from an authoritarian military regime in the 1990s, significantly reduced import tariffs for both CBU and CKD. The state relaxed restrictions on imports and started building linkages with foreign car assemblers to promote an outward-oriented economy (Tai & Ku, 2013). In Malaysia, tariffs for CKDs kits and auto parts were set between the range 40–50%, lower than those CBU tariffs. The obvious reason was to protect the local assemblers and encourage foreign automakers to use locally produced auto parts and kits.

The Malaysian government has set preferential treatment for the national carmakers. While a high tariff is imposed on CKDs for non-national cars, the government exempted 40% import tariff for Proton in 1985 and the exemption remained in effect until the early 1990s (Segawa et al., 2014). Later, the government set the tariff at only 13% in 1992 (this included the second national carmaker, Perodua) until

December 2003[2]. The national carmakers (Proton and Perodua) also enjoyed preferential treatment on excise duties. With the protective measures and privileges given to the national carmakers, Proton and Perodua had a competitive edge in terms of price over other foreign automakers in the Malaysian domestic market. In general, the Proton car is 50% lower than similar capacity cars produced by foreign car companies (Segawa et al., 2014) Furthermore, to ensure the national car has a strong market share in the domestic automobile industry, the government, through the Ministry of International Trade and Industry and its agency, the Malaysia Industrial Development Authority (MIDA), made arrangements (formally and informally) with other carmakers to limit the range of models that do not compete with Proton (Doner, 1992, pp. 110–111).

A non-tariff barrier is also used by the government to protect the domestic automotive sector. The Manufacturing Licensing (ML) is used to restrict imports on model and makes that do not constitute a direct challenge to the national carmakers, especially those non-national cars below 1800cc. As noted earlier, since the late 1960s the government introduced Approve Permit (AP) as an import quota, so most car dealers must apply for AP to import vehicles into the domestic market. The government used the AP as a quantitative restriction to limit the number of CBUs entering the domestic market during the early development of the automotive sectors (Mahidin & Kanageswary, 2004). To date, the AP is still used by the government but with minimal restriction, and the government agreed to phase out the franchise AP in 2020.

With strong support from the government, along with protective measures for the national carmakers, Proton (and later Perodua) manages to dominate the domestic automotive market. When the government introduced the first and second national car projects in 1985 and 1994, respectively, the WTO rules for most favoured nation had not been properly enforced. Under the General Agreement on Tariff and Trade (GATTS), there is a special consideration for infant industries by which the state can impose trade restrictions (both tariffs and quantitative restrictions) on a temporary basis, especially for a developing country (Michalopoulos, 2000, p. 6). In the case of Malaysia, the national automotive sector is deemed an infant industry. In addition, despite Southeast Asia committing to AFTA in 1992, the liberalisation effort only commenced after member countries came out with the Common Effective Preferential Tariff (CEPT) provision in 2002. However, Malaysia obtained an exemption to delay opening its automotive industry until 2006 (full implementation of CEPT was enforced in 2010).

---

[2]After 2005 all tariffs are set between 0 and 5%for CKD under the Asean Free Trade Agreement (AFTA). Further discussion will be made on this in Chapter 5.

3.3 Localisation Policy and Vendor Development

During the early development of the automotive industry, Most developing countries would adopt local content policy as part of protective measures for the local assemblers (Doner et al., 2004; Doner, 1992). In Southeast Asia, Malaysia, Thailand and Indonesia were the strong advocates for localisation policy during the formative years of the automotive industry (Doner, 1992; Abdulsomad, 1999). As noted in the early discussion on the Malaysian automotive industry, the government introduced two important localisation policies: the Mandatory Deletion Program in 1980 (MDP) and the Local Material Content Program (LMCP) in 1992. These policies are protective measures that set a minimum value of local parts and components that need to be sourced out to local suppliers (Rosli, 2006). The MDP proscribed from importing 30 parts and components listed under the program, while the LMCP required all automotive manufacturers to attain local content of up to 60% for passenger vehicles less than 1850cc, and 45% for passenger vehicles 1851cc–2850cc by 1996 (Tham, 2004, p. 55, see Fig. 4.4). The local content policy is applicable for both national car manufacturers and franchise approved permit holders of foreign automotive manufacturers (Alavi & Hasan, 2001) (Table 3.1).

After the localisation policy was introduced, the level of locally produced parts and components increased steadily from 8% in 1979 (before the national car project) to 30% in 1986. The impact of the policy can be seen in Proton. The first national car project is crucial in the localisation program to increase the locally produced parts and components for Proton. This is also to foster the local vendors as automobile components suppliers (Machado, 1994; Abdulsomad, 1999, p. 291). By the end of 1985, Proton's local content was around 20%, and the level of local content continued to increase from 40% in 1987 to 70% in 1989 (Meyanathan & Ismail, 1994). By 2002, local content constituted 80% in Proton and 65% in Perodua's passenger cars, whereas other passenger cars recorded 35–65% (Rosli, 2006). The number of locally sourced auto parts and components for Proton increased from 228 in 1985 to 1014 in

Table 3.1 Years of mandatory deletion program

Types of vehicles	1992 (%)	1993 (%)	1994 (%)	1995 (%)	1996 (%)	2002 (%)
Passenger vehicles <1,850cc	30	40	50	55	60	All Local content policy abolished
Passenger vehicles 1,850cc–2,850cc	20	30	35	40	45	
Passenger vehicles >2,850cc	Mandatory deletion items only					
Commercial vehicles <2,500cc						
Commercial vehicles >2,500cc						

Source Tham (2004)

1990, and the locally produced parts increased significantly to 4319 in 1998 (Alavi & Hasan, 2001; Segawa et al., 2014). Given the vast opportunity to engage in the national car supply chain, the number of vendors increased significantly from 17 in 1985 to 188 in 1998. By 2001, 350 vendors were created to supply parts and components in the automotive industry. For Perodua, there were 30 vendors in 2001 and the number increased to 135 in 2004. The large development of vendors in Malaysia under the localisation program mostly relied on national carmakers.

The government localisation program is linked to foster the development of local vendors. The localisation program provides opportunities to create backward linkages[3] for local vendors (Alavi & Hasan, 2001; Thoburn, 1973). Since the state plays strategic roles in facilitating the growth of the national car project, this makes it easier for the state to make linkages and arrangements to expand the vendor development. In Malaysia, where the state pays special consideration to Bumiputra to increase their involvement in economic development, they remain in consonance with the NEP objective to increase Bumiputra equity in commercial activities. This is one of the political manoeuvres used to create Bumiputra commercial and industrial community in order to strengthen the political base support for the long serving UMNO-led BN coalition government (Gomez & Jomo, 1997; Gomez, 2012, 2016). Scholars like Jomo (1994), Rasiah (1997), Bowie (1991), Gomez (2012) and Abdulsomad (1999) point out that This is one of the problems for national automotive industry, because implementing ethnic-coloured policy can reduce the efficiency and competitiveness of the national car project. The state-led development of the national car project generates economic rents, but those rents may be given to inexperienced firms that are politically connected.

In 1988, the government introduced the Vendor Development Program (VDP) to create greater industrial linkages between small and medium enterprises (SME) and large firms. The VDP was expected to be an important program to complement the localisation policy and support national automotive industries. The state guaranteed a market for products produced by vendors (Alavi & Hasan, 2001), hence Proton became the main anchor company for the program under the Proton Vendor Development Scheme (later this occurred with Perodua in 1994). While there are foreign firms participating in the program, the focus of the vendor development program is to foster Bumiputra small medium enterprise to be linked up in the national carmakers' supply chain (Sadoi, 1998; Rosli & Kari, 2008). This is part government strategy to increase the number of Bumiputra in auto kits manufacturing activities. Since the introduction of VDP, a considerable amount of funds is allocated for the development program in Malaysia through five-year plans and the Industrial Master Plan (I, II and III). The government's emphasis on Bumiputra participation in the automotive industry has created an artificial monopoly (Tan, 2008) in the production

[3] Alavi and Hasan (2001) posit that local content policy can foster greater backward linkages between industries where it can expand the volume or value of products because (i) close proximity with suppliers makes procurement cheaper, predictable, flexible and easier to negotiate and monitor, (ii) it is easier to provide technical information, product specification and material even when there is changes in production, (iii) there is lower risk of disruption of supplier, (iv) there is established trust and networking, (v) it can strengthen inter-firm relationships (p. 37).

of auto parts and components market for individual Bumiputra who are politically connected with the political elites.

Under the VDP that emphasises Bumiputra development, Proton is obliged to procure auto components preferentially from Bumiputra vendors,[4] despite the vendors having limited management and manufacturing experience. Proton employs a single sourcing system, meaning that only a single firm supplies a particular component. This system created rent, which intends to allow vendors to achieve economies of scales[5] and protect the vendors (Anazawa, 1997). The government also facilitates the local firms in 'match-making' to seek for partnerships with reputable foreign firms, in order to assist technology upgrading and skills development.[6] The partnership takes the form of joint-ventures, technical assistance programmes and purchase agreements. As a result, there is a rapid growth in the production of vehicles assembly and manufacturing in Malaysia. Demands for auto components have also increased. The Malaysia Industrial Development and Authority reported that there are about 300 firms in the auto parts, of which 70% engage in OEM production. At the same time, the number of Bumiputra vendors increased significantly, from 4 in 1985 to 142 in 2005 (PVA, 2005).

The localisation policy works similarly to tariff protection. This enables the state to protect local vendors and promote the vendor development program. The VDP has recorded success in developing automotive parts and components for SMEs and stimulating skills and technological development (Leutert & Sudhoff, 1999). However, the state-led vendor development has also had adverse consequences on the national automotive industry. The vendor program is less likely to 'pick up winners'; rather, it is driven by rent-seeking behaviour to obtain access to preferential treatment (Whah, 2012; Gomez & Jomo, 1997). Therefore, the state-led national automotive industry is unproductive because the rent is captured by inefficient producers (Rasiah, 1999), and it is difficult to replace those inefficient producers with productives one. Though the number of vendors increased over time, the firms linked to Proton failed to grow competitively. Most local suppliers are producing uneconomical scale, which leads to higher prices (Leutert & Sudhoff, 1999). The products of the auto kits tend to have inferior quality due to lack of quality control. The VDP has created fragmented industry structures with more than 300 firms producing different auto kits. Most of these firms are unable to achieve economies of scale that hinder technological upgrading. In contrast, suppliers that are not linked to VDP started to export and equipped their production process with higher-level technology (Leutert & Sudhoff, 1999). Knowing that a single-sourced system caused inefficiency, the national carmaker started to move away from the system by selecting competitive

[4]A vendor is considered Bumiputra if the SME shareholder fund is less than 2.5 million, 70% of the equity is held by Bumiputra, and 55% of the employees are Bumiputra.

[5]It was replaced by multisourcing in 2000 and phased out in 2005, after Malaysia committed to AFTA economic liberalisation.

[6]According to Paramjit (n.d.) after the match-making programme initiated by Proton for its vendors, 56% was with Japanese firms, 7% each with German and Korea firms, and 5% each with Taiwanese and French companies (cited in Alavi & Hasan, 2001, p. 42).

vendors in the Proton production network (Tham, 2014). However, this does not mean that the national carmaker can easily do away with the patronage system, because some politically-connected individuals remain as vendors to the national carmaker.

3.4 Liberalisation of Automotive Industry

Malaysia automotive sector has undergone changes since the 2000s. Pressure to change industrial policy has come from regional trade agreements (or other bilateral trade agreements) and commitments to international organisations, particularly the World Trade Organisation, which Malaysia has to comply with, the Most Favoured Nation tariff and national treatment policy principle (Tham, 2014; Natsuda & Thoburn, 2015). This pressure, embedded with pro-market oriented policy reforms, has somehow pushed the government to liberalise the domestic automotive market to make a freer business environment. Consequently, restrictive policy regime protecting the national car project has to be revised to promote a level playing field market environment.

As a founding member of the Association of Southeast Asia Nations, (ASEAN), Malaysia, along with the major Association of Southeast Asia Nations (ASEAN) members, namely Thailand, Indonesia, the Philippines and Singapore (later joined by Vietnam in 2006, Lao and Myanmar in 2008 and Cambodia in 2010), agreed to sign the ASEAN Free Trade Agreement (AFTA) in 1992 (Athukorala, 2014). The overarching objective of AFTA was to form regional trade liberalisation in Southeast Asia by 2008 (later re-schedule to 2003). Regional liberalisation is done to overcome the shortcoming in multilateral agreements in the WTO, especially for a developing country to negotiate terms of trade.[7] With the formation of AFTA, ASEAN member governments can position the region as a competitive base of production regionally and globally with their locational advantage. To this end, the ASEAN members come to collective agreements to promote intra-ASEAN trade and industrial linkages and specialisation, and to enhance economic efficiency, improve economies of scale and become a competitive production base for investment (ASEAN, 2015). AFTA can offer firms (local and foreign) greater access to a larger market and a wider base of resources in ASEAN countries.

This regional economic integration came out with a Common Effective Preferential Tariff (CEPT) provision in 2002. CEPT was introduced to help movement towards reducing existing tariffs and aimed to eliminate non-tariff barriers within ASEAN (Natsuda et al., 2013). Members of AFTA agreed to reduce tariffs applicable to imports within the region on 8,764 tariff lines, to between 0 and 5%. This was a major commitment made by the ASEAN members to liberalise the regional market. The global automakers operating in Southeast Asia expressed strong support

[7] This regionalist project enables member states to negotiate trade policy in more flexible manners and enhance cooperation between member states (Hurrell, 1995; Gamble & Payne, 1996)

on the regional liberalisation process. To facilitate negotiation between member countries and multinational automotive companies, the ASEAN Industrial Cooperation (AICO), a bilateral complementation scheme, launched in 1996. The AICO aims primarily to improve the auto industry in ASEAN countries with automakers in resource sharing pooling and industrial complementation (Doner, 2006a).

However, the automobile industry is not an easy policy agenda to deal with in the trade agreement, especially for Malaysia. Although CEPT was introduced in 2002 to provide a freer business environment in the ASEAN region, the actual full implementation was effectively enforced from 2010 onwards. This was because the Malaysian government attempted to delay the automotive trade liberalisation. The main reason was because the state has considerable interest in protecting the national car and its local parts and components producers. The Malaysian government pointed out that after the Asian Financial Crisis the national automotive industry had not recovered and the industry was still in its infant stage and needed more time to compete in an open environment (Mahidin & Kanageswary, 2004). The state has also been able to protect the automotive industry because it is also linked to Bumiputra interest, which is still unable to compete in a level playing field (Tan, 2008). Bumiputra interest is essential in economic policy as part of meeting the ethno-economic development and social engineering (Gomez, 2012; Wad, 2009). The elite policy-makers have to maintain domestic interests in automotive sectors. Though liberalisation can offer greater market access, this may not be the best interest of the elite policy-makers because it can undermine the national carmaker and its vendors.

The government requested that AFTA obtain exclusion for automobile products in the CEPT tariff reductions. Malaysia registered automobiles and production of parts and components on the Temporary Exclusion List (TEL) because it believed that the domestic automobile industry may face difficulties in the open market economy. This extension was granted in AFTA, though the Malaysian government had to reduce the tariff lines between 0 and 5% by 2005 (Tham, 2003). In contrast, Thailand, Indonesia and the Philippines, had transferred automobiles to the Inclusion List in 2000 under CEPT. In particular, Thailand intended to hasten the regional liberalisation process (especially for the automotive industry) because of vast foreign direct investments inflow from Japanese and European carmakers into the country (Kohpaiboon, 2008; Doner, 2006b).

Under CEPT, all ASEAN member governments agreed to effectively remove all tariff and non-tariff barriers in ASEAN countries that discriminate against automotive products that are considered 'Made in ASEAN' (Athukorala, 2014). CEPT results policy reforms for member states' trade policy, though for Malaysia such reforms potentially undermine the national interest, especially in automotive sectors. The pressure from AFTA to push for market reforms in the automotive industry seems inevitable for Malaysia. Commitment to trade liberalisation has made the government loosen some of its protective grip, as they had to make gradual tariff reductions and scale back quantitative imports restrictions in the automotive sector. The government made partial liberalisation manifest in the tariff reduction under CEPT in 2004, a year before the agreed deadline of 2005 (see Tables 3.2). Tariffs before liberalisation ranging from 70 to 190% had been reduced to 20% in 2005 for CBUs. Thereafter, they

Table 3.2 Tariffs on CBU

	Before 1997 (%)	1997 (%)	2004 (%)	2005 (%)	2006 (%)	2010 (%)
Engine capacity (cc) MFN Passenger vehicles						
<1,800	140	140	80	50	30[8]	30
≥1,800 to <2,000	170	170	100	50	30	30
≥2,000 to <2,500	170	200	120	50	30	30
≥2,500 to ≤3,000	200	250	160	50	30	30
>3,000	200	300	200	30	30	30
ASEAN (CEPT) Passenger vehicles						
<1,800	–	–	70	20	5	0
≥1,800 to <2,000	–	–	90	20	5	0
≥2,000 to <2,500	–	–	110	20	5	0
≥2,500 to ≤000	–	–	150	20	5	0
>3,000	–	–	190	20	5	0

decreased to 5% in 2006 and effectively cut to zero per cent in 2010. For CKDs, tariffs were removed in 2005. On the commitment to the WTO, under the Most Favoured Nation principle, tariffs initially set between 140 and 300% had been cut to 50% in 2005. Further reduction was made to 30% for all MFN CBUs, while for CKDs, tariffs were drastically cut from between 42 and 80% down to 10% (Table 3.3).

The market-oriented policy reforms have exposed the two national carmakers to competition from foreign automakers who have their production base in ASEAN countries, particularly in Thailand, the hub of most foreign automakers. The reforms also open up foreign carmakers, especially Japanese companies, to increase production on passenger cars, which potentially threatens the national carmaker's domestic market (Segawa et al., 2014). Prior to the trade liberalisation initiative, Proton managed to expand its total sales from 8,607 units in 1985 to reach a peak of 235,936 units in 1997. While Perodua also dominated the small size-car market segment with 63,225 units in 1997, the commendable growth in total number of sales for this second national car project, begun in 1994, was due to government support through tariffs. After the liberalisation process, the domestic market for the national car has changed drastically. Proton sales started to drop from 166,118 in 2005 to 115,538 in 2006. The combined market share of the two national carmakers declined from 92.7% in 2000 to 57.2% in 2010. The market share further shrank to 47.3% in 2015 for both national car companies. Proton has lost the position as the top selling car in Malaysia's market after the pro-market reforms. In fact, Proton's total sales in the domestic market have rarely reached more than 200,000 units after 2000. This was further compounded by the Great Recession in 2008 that caused decline in the total

[8] Malaysia applies the maximum tariff bound in WTO for automotive product

Table 3.3 Tariffs on CKD

	Before 1997 (%)	1997 (%)	2004 (%)	2005 (%)	2006 (%)	2010 (%)
Engine capacity (cc) MFN Passenger vehicles						
<1,800	42	42	35	50	10	10
≥1,800 to <2,000	42	42	35	50	10	10
≥2,000 to <2,500	42	60	35	50	10	10
≥2,500 to ≤3,000	42	70	35	50	10	10
>3,000	42	80	35	20	10	10
ASEAN CEPT Passenger vehicles						
<1,800	–	–	25	20	0	0
≥1,800 to <2,000	–	–	25	20	0	0
≥2,000 to <2,500	–	–	25	20	0	0
≥2,500 to ≤3,000	–	–	25	20	0	0
>3,000	–	–	25	20	0	0

Source Natsuda et al. (2012), MAI (2015)

market share of the national carmakers. In 2007, Proton recorded a loss of RM46.85 million (US$13.6 million) and increased to US$88.1 million (US$21.61 million) in 2011 (The Star, 2012; The Report, 2008). To date, Proton only manages to secure 15% of the domestic market. The company is also unable to resolve the overcapacity in their production, given that Proton is unable to capture a wider market share. Furthermore, the poor exports performance of Proton accounted for 16,189 units in 2011, followed by 13,311 units in 2012 and only 5,937 in 2015 (*Malay Mail*, 2014). This exports performance of around less than 10% of its total sales makes it unable to achieve economies of scales.

Perodua, the second national car project, is relatively resilient despite facing stiff competition from the international carmakers. This is partly because the company is managed by Daihatsu, which is associated with Toyota. Although there was a slight decline in terms of market share after the policy reforms, Perodua managed to maintain between 41.6% in 2006 and 32% in 2015. The second national car company tops the league for total sales in Malaysia's market after Proton. Although Perodua was able to capture the low-end of the car market, its exports performance is somehow better than Proton's but remains a suboptimal performance in the global market. Average export is between 10,000 units and 8,000 units, which is no more than 10% of its total sales (Harman, 2016). After the trade liberalisation, other Japanese companies and the European car market started to increase in Malaysia's domestic market. Japanese companies like Toyota, Honda, Nissan have gradually increased their market share, and Toyota and Honda have managed to reach more than 10% of it (Segawa et al., 2014). Previously, these auto carmakers were only able to capture less

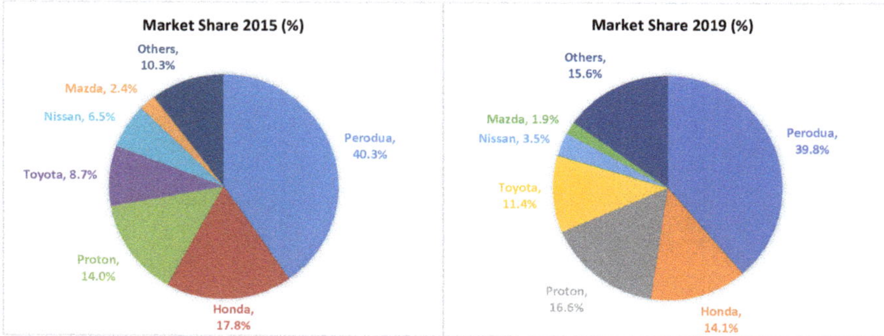

Fig. 3.1 Domestic automotive market share 2015 and 2019 (%) (*Source* MAA, 2016; MAI, 2019; Paultan, 2016)

than 10% of the domestic market share after the government imposed heavy tariffs in 1985. It is important to note that though the two national car projects may have lost market shares under open market competition, the national carmakers, especially Proton remains in the top three position in the overall market share in Malaysia (Fig. 3.1).

As mentioned in the earlier section, localisation policy introduced by the government is part of protective measures for local parts producers. The local content requirement imposed by developing countries is a contentious policy. The policy limits a freer business environment for foreign assemblers to operate in the host countries, which gives a greater role to the state to regulate the business environment. The policy obstructs the free business environment; thus it can affect economic efficiency and opportunities for international companies with multiple production plants for automobile parts and components. Malaysia, as a member of the WTO, was obliged to remove the policy by 2002 under the Trade Related Investment Measures (TRIMs).

Agreement on TRIMs was made after the Uruguay Round in 1994 and subsequently the establishment of the WTO (Tham, 2015). The agreement, referred to as a country investment policy, covers the conditions of investment relating to goods only. It acts as the core rules of the international trading regime by identifying measures of member governments that are not consistent with the national treatment, applying performance requirements (for instance it forces companies to use domestic inputs rather than imported inputs), and making quantitative restrictions (UNCTAD, 2006). Though the purpose of this agreement is to prevent the state from obstructing the free business environment, it does not restrict the host government from developing regulating measures for foreign companies. The agreement does not cover measures relating to technological transfer and export performance. Governments can still demand foreign firms to transfer technology by specifying certain portions of R&D locally or providing licenses for local firms on specific technology. Also, the host government can influence firms' employment practices with the aim to develop human capital, skills and training (UNCTAD, 2006; Shadlen,

2005; Natsuda & Thodurn, 2014). TRIMs can be categorised into to two types: 'positive,' for example when the state provides tax concessions to attract foreign investors, and 'negative', when governments can control foreign participation in certain sectors of the economy through the provision of tax incentives. This means that TRIMs provide options for a country to retain local content (Dunkley, 1997).

It is obvious, though, that the localisation policy used by the Malaysian government (including other ASEAN member states) violates TRIMs requirements. The local content policy limits business practices because it places obligations on foreign companies to procure locally made components and to limit the use of imported inputs. Under the TRIMs agreement, WTO member governments were given a time schedule to eliminate all measures. While developed countries were expected to remove them by 1997, developing countries were given until 2000 to remove policy that contravenes TRIMs. Malaysia's government started to phase out the local content program after it applied for two extensions. In 2002, the government agreed to remove the local content policy under the Local Material Content Program (LMCP) and removed 11 products from the Mandatory Deleted Items (MDI) list. The remaining 19 items listed in the MDI were abolished in 2004[9] (Alavi & Hasan, 2001, p. 35).

The government acquiesced to open up the automotive sector because liberalising the sector could threaten the national car project and local vendors in the domestic market. It could also undermine the growth of the national car to achieve economies of scale. The lacklustre export performance for both national carmakers do not contribute to the increase of total sales volume against the backdrop of the small domestic market. Similarly, the removal of local content policy could threaten the local vendors that are linked to Proton and Perodua. However, for the automotive industry to be competitive, the national car companies could not operate in a protective environment for a long period of time. This is because protective measures that lead to oligopolistic rents distort economic growth at the expense of consumer welfare, especially rents given to individuals with a strong political-cum-business interest under the rubric of national champion. It is necessary to open the domestic automotive market so that the national car companies would strive for better quality products, improve labour skills and create incentives for innovation in a level playing field environment (Rasiah, 1997; Tham, 2014).

3.5 National Automotive Policy (NAP)

After the liberalisation pressure, the government introduced the National Automotive Policy (NAP) in 2006 to promote the competitiveness of Malaysia's automotive industry. NAP is the main thrust in Malaysia's third Industrial Master Plan (IMP 3 2006–2020). After the liberalisation initiative, the government started to craft the

---

[9]While most Southeast Asian countries have removed local content policy but under AFTA member' states agreed to have tariff cut between 0 and 5% tariff. Nevertheless, it has to meet 40% local content requirement originating from participating ASEAN countries

national automotive policy as part of its response to the liberalisation pressure. NAP was introduced in 2006 with two revisions in 2009 and 2014. The overarching objective of NAP is to transform the domestic automotive industry and integrate it into the regional and global industry network, within the increasingly liberalised and competitive global environment (MITI, 2006a). The policy also laid down six objectives to strengthen the national automotive industry: (i) to promote a competitive and sustainable domestic automotive industry, especially for national car manufacturers; (ii) to develop Malaysia as a regional automotive hub; (iii) to enhance value added and local capabilities in the industry; (iv) to promote the export of vehicles and automotive components; (v) to promote Bumiputra participation in the industry; and (vi) to safeguard consumer interests by offering safer and better quality products.

In 2009, the policy was revised to further enhance the capability and competitiveness of the domestic automotive sectors in response to increasing liberalisation pressure and changes in the global automotive industry. The government attempted to attract investment in high technology sectors such as electric and hybrid vehicle production (MIDA, 2010). The revised NAP in 2009 was not much different than the initial NAP, except the government introduced more incentives for foreign companies to promote high tech and value-added activities. The underlying reason was to build linkages with Bumiputra vendors to improve competitiveness. In 2014, the government revised the NAP again by putting emphasis on green initiatives in order to become a regional hub in energy efficient vehicles (EEV) as part of market expansion and to attract more foreign investors.[10] The shift to green initiatives can be associated with the success of the 'eco-car' in Thailand, which provides lucrative tax privileges and excises duty rebates for foreign assemblers and suppliers (Doner & Wad, 2014).

After the change of government in 2018, Prime Minister Mahathir launched the latest version of NAP 2020. Mahathir who is also responsible for the development of national automotive industry, laid down new objectives for NAP 2020. The policy envisions to enhance Malaysia's automotive industry in the era of digital industrial transformation from 2020 to 2030, thus enabling Malaysia to realise Connected Mobility. Even though Malaysia automotive industry fall short in achieving its NAP 2014 as EEV hub, now the new government has to push the industry to embrace the rapidly changing environment in automotive industry in tandem with Big Data Analytics, Internet of Things, Artificial Intelligence (AI) and alternative fuel powertrains have changed the landscape of the industry as they bring new aspects and offerings to vehicle development (NAP, 2020). In line with the NAP 2020, new Malaysia Vehicle Project or Third National Car Project will be introduced. Despite there are so many shortcomings for two national car projects (Proton and Perodua), the government plans to come out with third national car project with full private initiative. This project will work along with NAP 2020 objectives. More importantly to develop supply chain that work along with Next Generation Vehicle and Industrial Revolution 4.0

[10]In 2014, the government added two objectives to the National Automotive Policy: (i) to develop Malaysia as the regional automotive hub in Energy Efficient Vehicles (EEV) and (ii) to enhance the ecosystem of the manufacturing and after-market sectors of the domestic automotive industry.

The NAP (2009, 2014, 2016, 2020) retains its stance to adopt a market-based economy policy. Undoubtedly, pro market reform is essential to drive technological advancement to make domestic automotive industry more competitive. In the policy, the government acknowledges issues related to problems in the domestic automotive industry such as low economies of scale, high production costs, low usage of technology and knowledge application, non-optimised supply chains and development of human capital (NAP, 2014). In view of these challenges, the government aimed to address mainly new investment in specific sections of the automotive industry (for example, in hybrid and electrical cars, Next Generation Vehicle, Mobility as Service, incorporating Big Data Analytics (BDA), Internet of Things, Smart manufacturing), market expansion (partnership with foreign companies), moving up the supply value chain, improvement of technology and development (this includes R&D and disruptive technology), and human capital development.

Considering the tariff was already reduced considerably, institutional arrangements were made in the policy to enhance competitiveness in the domestic automotive industry by the government opening up the Manufacturing License (ML) for manufacturing and assembling activities. The government provided tax incentives such as the Pioneer Status of 100% fiscal reduction for 10 years and the Investment Tax Allowance of 100% for five years, for foreign companies that promote high value-added production on parts and components (NAP, 2009). This includes investment in hybrid and electric vehicles to attract more OEMs to move their operations into Malaysia. Among other non-tariff barriers in Malaysia's automotive industry, the Approve Permits (AP) were import quota permits introduced in the late 1960s as part of the redistributive programme under NEP. AP was introduced to facilitate Bumiputra participation in the automotive industry. There are two types of AP: open AP, which is an import permit for used vehicles, and franchise AP, which deals with producers of new vehicles that have equity condition. Since non-tariff barriers can distort the automotive market, in the NAP the government set to phase out the open AP system by 31 December 2015 in order to gradually eliminate the imported used cars that could potentially undermine the CBUs in the domestic market. The government also committed to remove the franchise AP by 31 December 2020 (MITI, 2014).

One of the significant elements in the NAP to enhance the competitiveness of the national car manufacturer is the aim to form a strategic partnership between Proton and global automotive producers. This is part of the economic transformation program under Najib's administration to strengthen the position of the national car in the automotive production network through a private-led initiative. Wad and Govindaraju (2011) observe that the government attempts to retreat from the national car project that they cannot handle by having partnerships that could at least address the large idle capacity of Proton. Furthermore, the government introduced the Malaysia Automotive Institute (MAI) in 2010, a newly established government agency that provides resources to assist domestic automotive development (technology, marketing and management) including for the local vendors. This agency can help facilitate resources gaps for national car marker and local vendors and coordinate linkages with other OEMs. The intention of the NAP was to advocate strategic partnerships that enable the national carmaker to be competitive, address long-term viability, access the latest technology (including technology transfer) and, more importantly, enable Malaysia to play a major role as a regional hub for the automotive industry by increasing exports (Natsuda et al., 2013; MITI, 2009). However, forming strategic partnerships remains questionable in the NAP due to Bumiputra and other political interests linked to Proton (Nehru, 2012).

Although the NAP adopts a pro-market oriented approach, the liberalisation of the domestic automotive industry is not done straightforwardly. While the Malaysian government has reduced tariffs under AFTA and WTO obligation, new excise duty has been introduced as a way to protect the national carmaker (see Table 3.4). The government imposes excise duties between 75 and 105% for imported CBUs and CKDs components. The tax structure is considered the highest in the ASEAN

Table 3.4 Excise tax in Malaysia

	CBU vehicles			CKD component		
	Tariff (%)	Excise duty (%)	Sales tax (%)	Tariff (%)	Excise duty (%)	Sales tax (%)
Engine capacity (cc) MFN Passenger vehicles						
<1800	30	75	10	10	75	10
≥1800 to <2000	30	80	10	10	80	10
≥2000 to <2500	30	90	10	10	90	10
≥2500 to ≤3000	30	105	10	10	105	10
>3000	30	105	10	10	105	10
ASEAN (CEPT) Passenger vehicles						
<1,500	0	60	10	0	60	10
1,500 to <1,800	0	65	10	0	65	10
≥1,800 to <2,000	0	75	10	0	75	10
≥2,000 to <2,500	0	90	10	0	90	10
≥2,500 to ≤3,000	0	105	10	0	105	10

Source Malaysia Automotive Institute (2019)
Note Effective 1st April 2015 government will introduce Goods and Service Tax (GST) 6% which will replace the existing Sales and Service Tax. GST is a value added tax therefore it applies at each stage of the business transaction, from manufacturer, distribution, retail and to the consumer. It is expected to increase car prices including national cars

region[11] (Peerson, 2015). The national cars are given 50% exemption from excise duty (Jomo, 2007), and although the exemption was due to expire in 2004, the government continues to provide the tax exemption for the national car (Reuters, 2004). The excise duties discriminate prices between national and non-national cars, which inflates non-national car prices. In short, the excise duty provides a decisive cost advantage for the national cars so that they are able to maintain sales in the market. It is estimated that Proton would be significantly more expensive if it had to compete in a level playing field with global brands, especially with Japanese automakers (Fujita, 1999; Nehru, 2012).

The Malaysia government continues to maintain non-tariff barriers to shield the domestic automotive industries. The government relaxed the issuance of manufacturing licenses F as part of opening up the domestic automotive market. However, ML will be given only to certain segments of the vehicle production, notably to the assembling of luxury passenger cars with an engine capacity of 1800cc and above, and with price of no less than RM150,000. ML will also be issued to motor vehicle hybrids and electrical vehicles (including with EEV category), pick-up trucks and commercial vehicles (MITI, 2009; MACPMA, 2008; NAP, 2014). Although the government partially relaxed its non-tariff barriers, it tries to limit the import of foreign cars that constitute a direct threat to national carmakers. In particular, this applies to vehicle products for 1600cc (and below) and small size engine vehicles, the market segment dominated by the national car. This means institutional arrangement is made among policy actors in the NAP to support the national car project.

The government continues the open AP system as one of the non-tariff barriers to limit numbers of imported CKDs and CBUs. Initially when the government introduced the NAP in 2006, the AP system was scheduled to be removed in 2010 but was differed until December 2015. However, in 2015 the government decided to continue the open AP until 1 January 2017. The Minister of International Trade and Industry stated that the decision to postpone the open AP system was because the business of imports and distributions of imported used cars have contributed significantly to the automotive industry and to socio-economic development. This included contribution to other service sectors (banking, insurance, shipping and logistics) and generating employment opportunities. To abolish the AP system is difficult because such economic rents are captured by politically linked individuals (Lim, 2005). These individuals can threaten any individuals or business groups that attempt remove the special import permits. AP has the same impact on import quotas, which can cause distortion in the domestic market (WTO, 2012). To reduce this impact, under the NAP the government attempts to streamline the AP system by limiting the number of AP holders. An in-depth audit will be implemented to ensure APs are not misused by individuals. New applicants for AP have to prove having minimum paid up capital of RM1 million[12] and a ready premise to operate auto dealership (MITI, 2016). New

[11] Excise tax for both CBUs and CKD in Thailand is between 25 and 50%, in Indonesia it is between 20 and 75% and in the Philippines it is between 15 and 100%. The excise duties depend on the engine sizes (Peerson, 2015).

[12] Full details of the AP requirement can be assessed in MITI website.

application for open AP requires a payment of RM10,000 for each permit, money which will be channelled to the Bumiputra Automotive Development Fund as part of assisting Bumiputra companies venturing into the automotive industry and other businesses (MIDA, 2012).

Despite the fact that the NAP is an attempt to liberalise the domestic automotive market, the Bumiputra agenda still constitutes an important part of it. Theoretically, emphasising certain ethnic group development is inconsistent with the neoliberal approach, because giving preferential treatment to certain ethnic groups defeats the purpose of equal access to compete for resources in the policy (Ho, 1988; Whah, 2012, Aun, 2002). It also creates an unlevel playing field due to artificial distortion formed by the state. Such affirmative action policy could further create rent-seeking behaviour among the groups to obtain access to state resources (Khan, 2000). When ethno-development retains an agenda in the automotive industry, the government could maintain the patronage system in the industry to ensure Bumiputra vendors can benefit from such policy (Gomez, 2009, 2016). In fact, the affirmative action policy was under scrutiny under Najib's economic transformation plan and there was a move to reduce the emphasis on it; that is, to do away with Bumiputra policy because ethnic-based development had slowed industrial development (Fauzi & Takiyuddin, 2014; Tan, 2010). Najib's administration intended to replace the ethnics-based policy to a need-based one irrespective of race. Fauzi and Takiyuddin (2014) observe that the government attempts to allow private-led development in an attempt to scale down the role of the state in the market. When Najib announced the decision to end the Bumiputra policy (The Star, 2009), there was mounting pressure from the UMNO right wing, including Mahathir Mohammad (Proton's advisor), which forced him to re-institute the Bumiputra policy (Gomez, 2016). Thus the NAP remains the emphasis of Bumiputra participation in the automotive industry. Special funds are allocated to increase the Bumiputra role in automotive industries.

Under the NAP the government has not completely withdrawn their protection for local vendors. There are several measures in the NAP to ensure the sustainable development of the national car and local producers of auto kits and components. As mentioned earlier, the government has phased out the localisation policy, however, it is not done straightforwardly. The obvious method in the NAP is that the government provides tax exemption for companies that promote exports with a significant portion of the assembly activities value added in Malaysia. Tax exemption is given based on the percentage in the values assembly in Malaysia.[13] The tax exemption policy does not force companies to source locally made auto parts and components like the previous local content policy, but rather encourages assemblers to procure from the local firms with tax exemptions.

The NAP states that the government will continue to provide institutional support for local firms, including financial (soft loans & grants) and non-financial support, so that vendors that are linked to national carmakers can grow in the competitive market.

[13]Tax exemption on statutory income for assemblers is enhanced from 10 to 30% of the value of increased exports, provided the goods attain at least 30% value added, and from 15 to 50% of values of increased exports provided that the goods attain at least 50% value added (see MITI, 2016).

Among other measures introduced in the NAP to encourage growth of the local automotive firms are the Industrial Adjustment Fund, the Automotive Development Fund and the Industrial Development Linkages (NAP, 2014). These measures may not obstruct a freer business environment in domestic automotive sectors, but they are instruments devised by the state to facilitate the domestic automotive industry, especially national carmakers and local vendors linked to them. The Industrial Adjustment Fund (IAF)[14] is a fund given to a company to strengthen a particular sector (in this case automotive sectors) and can be linked to local content. The IAF works to enable assemblers to receive incentives (for example, interest free loans and grants) based on scale and industry linkages, upgrading of machinery, component development costs and technology enhancements (MITI, 2006a). Assemblers that engage in such activities to facilitate the local vendors will have access to state grants and financial supports. Furthermore, assemblers that promote competitive Bumiputra in the automotive industry will obtain IAF. Proton and Perodua are the main beneficiaries of the IAF.

Similar to the IAF is the Industrial Linkages Program (ILP) introduced under the NAP. The ILP is a program initiated by the government to link local vendors and foreign companies as part of facilitating vendor engagement in the foreign companies' supply chains (UNCTAD, 2013). Vendors that are linked to foreign assemblers are required to manufacture products or undertake activities in the List of Promoted Activities and Products in the ILP. This can be linked to the local content requirement, because foreign assemblers working with local vendors can obtain excise tax according to the values of locally procure. The ILP requires assemblers to source auto parts from vendors that are part of the Proton Vendor Association, Perodua Vendor Association or Malaysia Automotive Components Parts Association (MACPMA). The Automotive Development Fund (ADF) is akin to a fiscal stimulus fund. The ADF aims to rationalise and strengthen local vendors' competitiveness by providing low interest loans. The loan is to facilitate local vendors in improving production activities and upgrading. Also, ADF facilitates the merger and acquisition of weaker vendors due to the reduction of the CKDs tariff. Similarly, the ADF is given mainly to the Proton or Perodua vendor's associations. This is part of the aim to facilitate Bumiputra development in order to be competitive in the automotive industry (MAI, 2015).

[14]Industrial Adjustment is defined as any activity of a company operating in a sector within the manufacturing industry to restructure the company by way of reorganisation, reconstruction or amalgamation within that particular sector, with a view towards strengthening the basis for industrial self-sufficiency, improving industrial technology, increasing productivity, and enhancing the efficient use of natural resources and manpower management (MITI, 2017 see factsheets—incentive for industrial adjustment fund).

3.6 Conclusion

The Malaysian automotive industry is one of the main segments of industrial development owing to the complex wide industrial linkages. Prior to the introduction of the national car project, there were many government initiatives to facilitate the growth of national automotive sectors, such as localisation policy and the controversial Approve Permits (AP). As part of diversifying the industrial structure of the automotive sector, the government introduced the national car projects despite lacking industrial expertise. By pursuing the national car project, the government was able to rationalise the automobile industry, promote related industry, enhance utilisation of locally-made components, encourage upgrading of technology, and also spur the industrialisation process. High tariff and non-tariff barriers were erected to protect the domestic automotive sector and national car projects. This was to enable national cars to grow in the marketplace, while at the same time restricting other auto companies' makes and models.

The political elite had also fashioned the national car project as a nationalist economic project in order to increase Bumiputra participation. This was inevitable, because the NEP has become a 'guiding principle' to incorporate the Bumiputra agenda. The direction of the national car projects and other policies associated with the development of the national automotive industry shows the capacity of ruling elite in modernising the automotive industry. This gives a paternalistic role to the ruling elites in the automotive market as they are able to provide preferential treatment to the local car companies and the vendor development programme. While dependence on state resources at the outset of industrial development is crucial for national carmakers and the vendor development programme, ongoing dependence on rents may have detrimental effects on the automotive sector. Furthermore, the lack of strict performance requirement left in place has led the local carmakers and other vendors to be less competitive.

The outcome of the NAP is seen as the government adopts a more open economy in its automotive sector, which has been protected since the formation of the national car project. A pro-market oriented policy reform in Malaysia's domestic automotive industry seems inevitable. Liberalising the domestic automotive industry is crucial to expand market access, productivity gain, technological advancement and capital accumulation. Other ASEAN member states have started opening up their automotive sectors, given the potential of the sectors to expand and improve manufacturing activities. However, in the case of Malaysia, opening up the market could undermine the national car project that is embedded with state interests. The country cannot operate in a protective environment for a long period of time, though, because this may limit market access, productivity gain and growth. There is a need to liberalise the domestic automotive industry. The policy arrangements made by policy actors are unlikely to make the national car competitive in a level playing field or undermine the local vendor interests.

While the NAP is seen as a pro-market oriented policy reform to constitute a level playing field for other automakers in the Malaysian market, the policy is coordinated to protect the domestic automotive sector. Despite the poor performance of sales and exports, the policy seeks to preserve the interest of the national carmakers. Institutional arrangements are made by the state elites and industrial groups to continue to facilitate the national carmaker in the market and to preserve local vendor interests. The government's interests are entrenched in the institutional arrangements, making it difficult to pursue a market-based policy. As a result of the arrangements, the policy is crafted to shield the domestic automotive industry, such as by imposing a high excise duty. Low tariffs imposed on imported CBUs and CKDs, licenses and approved permits still exist as non-tariff barriers to limit imported cars that directly threaten national cars, maintaining the localisation policy and special funds for the national car projects and the local vendors. By incorporating Bumiputra interest in the NAP as one way to protect the national car project, the state elites can mobilise more state resources to secure the growth of the sector in terms of 'national interest'.

The historical specificity of the development of automotive sectors may affect the growth of the automotive industry and the automotive policy. The dependence of national car and vendors on state rents to grow at the outset will not be easy to remove in the long run. Underpinned by the patron-client network, rent-seeking behaviour will continue, especially when the development of the automotive industry is linked to industrial nationalism and Bumiputra class interest.

References

Abdulsomad, K. (1999). Promoting industrial and technological development under contrasting industrial policies: The automotive industry in Malaysia and Thailand. In K. S. Jomo, G. Felker, & R. Rasiah (Eds.), *Industrial technology development in Malaysia: Industry and firm studies*. New York: Routledge.

Alavi, R., & Hasan, S. (2001). The impact of TRIMs on Malaysian automotive SME vendors. *Kajian Malaysia, 19*(2), 27–60.

Anazawa, M. (1997). Technology transfer in the automobile industry in Malaysia: PROTON and vendors. *Economic Review, 47*(4), 119–154.

ASEAN Automotive Association. (2015). *ASEAN automotive federation statistics 2015*. http://www.asean-autofed.com/statistics.html.

Athukorala, P. C. (2014). *Industrialisation through state-MNC partnership: Lesson from Malaysia national car project* (Arndt-Corden Department of Economics, Crawford School of Public Policy, Working Paper No. 2014/06).

Aun, L. H. (2002). *Industrial development and equity distribution in Malaysia manufacturing: Institutional perspectives* (Working Paper Series Centre on Regulation and Competition University of Manchester Automotive Industry). https://ideas.repec.org/p/ags/idpmcr/30659.html.

Bartu, F. (1992). *The ugly Japanese: Nippon's economic empire in Asia*. Singapore: Longman.

Bowie, A. (1991). *Crossing the industrial divide: State, society and the politics of economic transformation in Malaysia*. New York: Columbia University Press.

Doner, F. R., & Wad, P. (2014). Financial crisis and automotive industry development in Southeast Asia. *Journal of Contemporary Asia, 44*(4), 664–687.

Doner, R. F. (1992). Limits of state strength: Toward an institutionalist view of economic development. *World Politics, 44*(3), 398–431.

Doner, R. F. (2006a). *Automotive industry development in East Asia: Performance, politics and institutions.* Paper presented at the 2006 meeting of the International Studies Association, San Dieago, CA.

Doner, R. F. (2006b). *Industrial competitiveness of the auto parts industry in four large Asian countries: The role of government policy in a challenging international environment* (World Bank Policy Research Report no. 4106).

Doner, R., Noble, G. W., & Ravenhill, J. (2004). Production network in East Asia's automobile parts industry. In S. Yusuf, M. A. Altaf, & K. Nabeshima (Eds.), *Global production networking and technological change in East Asia.* World Bank and Oxford University Press.

Dunkley, G. (1997). *The free trade adventure: The WTO, the Uruguay Round and globalism—A critique.* London: Zed Books.

Embong, A. R. (1996). Social transformation, the state and the middle classes in post-independence Malaysia. *Southeast Asia Studies, 34*(3).

Embong, A. R. (2012). Developmental state capacity and institutional reforms. In B. T. Khoo (Eds.), *Policy regimes and political economy of poverty reduction in Malaysia.* United Nations Research Institute for Social Development UNRISD.

Fauzi, A., & Takiyuddin, I. M. (2014). Malaysia's general elections amidst the shadow of re-Mahathirisation. *Kajian Malaysia, 32*(2), 1–24.

Fujita, M. (1999). *Industrial policies and trade Liberalization: The automotive industry in Thailand and Malaysia.* APEC Study Center Institute of Developing Economies.

Gamble, A., & Payne, A. (1996). Conclusion: The new regionalism. In A. Gamble & A. Payne (Eds.), *Regionalism and world order* (pp. 247–264). London: Macmillan.

Gomez, E. T. (2009). The rise and fall of capital: Corporate Malaysia in historical perspectives. *Journal of Contemporary Asia, 39*(3), 345–381.

Gomez, E. T. (2016). Resisting the fall: The single dominant party, policies and elections in Malaysia. *Journal of Contemporary Asia.*

Gomez, E. T., & Jomo, K. S. (1997). *Malaysia's political economy: politics, patronage and profits.* Cambridge: Cambridge University Press.

Gomez, T. (2012). The politics and policies of corporate development: Race, rent and redistribution in Malaysia. In H. Hill, S. Y. Tham, & M. Z. Ragayah (Eds.), *Malaysia development challenges: Graduating from the middle.* New York: Routledge.

Harman, A. (2016). Proton quits some global markets amid export slump. *WardsAuto.* http://wardsauto.com/industry/proton-quits-some-global-markets-amid-export-slump.

Hasan, H., & Jomo, K. S. (2007). Rent-seeking and industrial policy in Malaysia. In K. S. Jomo (Ed.), *Malaysia industrial policy.* Singapore: NUS Press.

Ho, K. L. (1988) *Indigenising the state: The NEP and Bumiputra state in peninsular Malaysia.* Ohio State University. https://www.pressreader.com/malaysia/the-star-malaysia/20120411/282591669924326.

Hurrell, A. (1995). Regionalism in theoretical perspective. In F. Louise & H. Andrew (Eds.), *Regionalism in world politics* (pp. 3–73). Oxford: Oxford University Press.

Jayasankaran, S. (1994). Made in Malaysia: The Proton project. In K. S. Jomo (Ed.), *Japan and Malaysian development—In the shadow of the rising sun.* London: Routledge.

Jomo, K. S. (Ed.). (1993). *Industrializing Malaysia: Policy, performance, prospects.* Routledge.

Jomo, K. S. (1994). The Proton Saga: Malaysian car, Mitsubishi gain. In K. S. Jomo (Ed.), *Japan and Malaysian development—In the shadow of the rising sun.* London: Routledge.

Jomo, K. S. (2007). Industrialisation and industrial policy in Malaysia. In K. S. Jomo (Ed.), *Malaysia industrial policy.* Singapore: NUS Press.

Jomo, K. S., & Wee, C. H. (2014). *Malaysia@50: Economic development, distribution and disparities.* Strategic Information and Research Development Malaysia.

Kanapthy, V. (2001). Industrial restructuring in Malaysia: Policy shifts and the promotion of new sources of growth. In M. Seiichi, V. C. Donna & C. S, Yue (Eds.), *Industrial restructuring in East Asia: Towards the 21st century.* Tokyo: Nomura Research Institute.

Khan, M. (2000). Rents, rent-seeking and economic development: An introduction. In M. Khan (Ed.). *Rent, rent-seeking and economic development: Theory and evidence in Asia.* Cambridge University Press.

Kohpaiboon, A. (2008). *Thai automotive industry: Multinational enterprises and global integration* (*Economic* Research and Training Centre Thailand, Discussion Paper No. 0004).

Lall, S. (2000). The technological structure and performance of developing country manufactured exports, 1985–98. *Oxford Development Studies, 28*(3), 337–369.

Leutert, H. G., & Sudhoff, R. (1999). Technology capacity building in the Malaysian automotive industry. In K. S. Jomo, G. Felker, & R. Rasiah (Eds.), *Industrial technology development in Malaysia: Industry and firm studies.* New York: Routledge.

Lim, K. S. (2005). *Who is the king of APs? Making public AP holders in the national interest.* Parliament speech. https://dapmalaysia.org/all-archive/English/2005/jun05/lge/lge131.htm.

Machado, K. G. (1994). Proton and Malaysia's motor vehicle industry: National industries policy and Japanese regional production strategies. In K. S. Jomo (Ed.), *Japan and Malaysian development—In the shadow of the rising sun.* London: Routledge.

Mahidin, M. U., & Kanageswary, R. (2004). The development of automotive industry and the road ahead. *Journal of Department of Statistic Malaysia, 2,* 1–32.

Malay Mail. (2014). Proton will review export strategy, says Mustapa. http://www.themalaymail online.com/money/article/proton-will-review-export-strategy-says-mustapa#xqjdo8yr5i67lMq k.99.

Malaysia Automotive Association (MAA). (2016). Malaysia Automotive Info: Summary of sales and production data. http://www.maa.org.my/info_summary.htm.

Malaysia Automotive Institute (MAI). (2015). Press release. http://newswire.mai.org.my/.

Malaysia Automotive Institute (MAI). (2019). Press release. http://newswire.mai.org.my/.

Malaysia Investment Development Authority (MIDA). (2010). Business opportunity: Malaysia.

Malaysia Investment Development Authority (MIDA). (2012). *Malaysia's automotive industry.* http://www.mida.gov.my/env3/uploads/Publications_pdf/BO_MalaysiaAutomotive/Automotiv e2012.pdf.

Malaysian Automotive Component Parts Manufacturers Associations (MACPMA). (2008). Malaysian automotive component parts manufacturers directory.

Mehmet, O. (1999). Malaysia after Mahathir. In B. N. Ghosh & M. S. Salleh (Eds.), *Political economy of development in Malaysia.* Malaysia: Utusan Publication and Distribution Sdn Bhd.

Menon, J. (2008). *Macroeconomic management amid ethnic diversity: Fifty years of Malaysian experience* (ADB Institute Discussion Paper No. 102).

Meyanathan, S. D., & Ismail, M. S. (1994). Malaysia. In S. D. Meyanathan (Ed.), *Industrial structures and the development of small and medium enterprise linkages: Examples from East Asia.* Washington, DC: World Bank.

Michalopoulos, C. (2000). *Trade and development in the GATT and WTO: The rile of special and differential treatment for developing countries.* World Trade Organisation.

Ministry of International Trade and Industry (MITI). (2006a). *Third industrial master plan.* http://www.miti.gov.my/miti/resources/fileupload/contents.pdf.

Ministry of International Trade and Industry (MITI) Malaysia. (2006b). *Investments in the manufacturing and services sectors.* http://www.miti.gov.my/miti/resources/fileupload/Chap%204.pdf.

Ministry of International Trade and Industry (MITI) Malaysia. (2009). *Industrial adjustment fund.* http://www.miti.gov.my/index.php/pages/view/1449.

Ministry of International Trade and Industry Malaysia (MITI). (2014). *Review of National Automotive Policy: MITI advances the Government of Malaysia's agenda of liberalisation, paving the way for a more competitive automotive industry for domestic, regional and global markets.* http://www.miti.gov.my/index.php/pages/view/1449.

Ministry of International Trade and Industry (MITI) Malaysia. (2016). Approve permit. http://www.miti.gov.my/index.php/pages/view/2096.

Ministry of International Trade and Industry (MITI) Malaysia. (2017). Factsheet incentive for industrial adjustment fund. http://www.recoda.com.my/wp-content/uploads/2017/11/SCORE_factsheet-incentivesforindustrialadjustment.pdf.

National Automotive Policy (NAP). (2009). Available http://www.maa.org.my/pdf/NAP_2019_policy.pdf.

National Automotive Policy (NAP). (2014). Available http://www.maa.org.my/pdf/NAP_2014_policy.pdf.

National Automotive Policy (NAP). (2016). Available http://www.maa.org.my/pdf/NAP_2019_policy.pdf.

National Automotive Policy (NAP). (2020). https://www.miti.gov.my/index.php/pages/view/nap2020

Natsuda, K., & Thoburn, J. (2014). How much policy space still exists under the WTO? A comparative study of the automotive industry in Thailand and Malaysia. *Review of International Political Economy, 21*(6), 1346–1377.

Natsuda, K., & Thoburn, J. (2015). How much policy space still exists under the WTO? A comparative study of the automotive industry in Thailand and Malaysia. *Review of International Political Economy, 21*(6), 1346–1377.

Natsuda, K., Segawa, N., & Thoburn, J. (2012). Globalisation and the Malaysia automotive industry: Industrial nationalism, liberalisation and the role of Japan. *Global Economic Review, 42*(2).

Natsuda, K., Segawa, N., & Thoburn, J. (2013). Globalisation and the Malaysia automotive industry: industrial nationalism, liberalisation and the role of Japan. *Global Economic Review, 42*(2).

Nehru, V. (2012, March 22). Modern industrial policy: Lesson from Malaysia's auto industry. *International Economic Bulletin*. http://www.carnegieendowment.org/ieb/2012/03/22/modern-industrial-policy-lessons-from-malaysia-s-auto-industry/a4cr.

Paramjit, S. (n.d.). The Malaysian automotive industry. *ASEAN Auto Datebase*. www.aseanauto.org/mal/report.htm.

Paultan. (2016). Malaysia vehicle sales data for May 2015 by brand. https://paultan.org/2015/06/23/malaysia-vehicle-sales-data-for-may-2015-by-brand/.

Peerson, R. (2015). Automotive excise taxation: What reforms are needed to best utilise the ASEAN Economic Community? *World Custom Journal, 9*(1).

Proton Vendor Association (PVA). (2005). *Proton Vendor's Directory*.

Rasiah, R. (1997). Rent in Proton management. In M. Khan & K. S. Jomo (Eds.), *Rents and development*. Cambridge University Press.

Rasiah, R. (1999). *Liberalization and the car industry in Southeast Asia*, Department of Intercultural Communication and Management, Copenhagen Business School.

Reuters. (2004). *Automotive news: Malaysian carmaker Proton says halts sales slide*. http://www.autonews.com/article/20041021000100/REG/410210718?template=print.

Rosli, M. (2006). The automobile industry and performance of Malaysia auto production. *Journal of Economic Cooperation, 27*(1), 88–114.

Rosli, M., & Kari, F. (2008). *The comparative performance of local and foreign suppliers in the Malaysian automotive industry: the case of Proton's vendor*. Paper presented at the International Conference on Foreign Direct Investment and Technology Transfer in Asia, AEI/UM, Kuala Lumpur, Malaysia.

Sadoi, Y. (1998). Skill formation in Malaysia: The case of auto parts industry. *Department Bulletin Paper*, Kyoto University Research Information Repository.

Segawa, N., Natsuda, K., & Thoburn, J. (2014). Affirmative action and economic liberalisation: The dilemmas of the Malaysian automotive industry. *Asian Studies Review, 38*(3), 422–441.

Shadlen, K. C. (2005). Exchanging development for market access? Deep integration and industrial policy under multilateral and regional-bilateral trade agreements. *Review of International Political Economy, 12*(5), 750–775.

Tai, W. P., & Ku, S. C. Y. (2013). State and industrial policy: Comparative political economic analysis of automotive industrial policies in Malaysia and Thailand. *Journal of ASEAN, 1*(1), 55–82.

Tan, J. (2008) *Privatisation in Malaysia: Regulation, rent-seeking and policy failure.* Routledge.

Tan, J. (2010, June 6). All ears to the Malay voice. *The Sunday Star.*

Tan, J. (2014). Running out of steam? Manufacturing in Malaysia. *Cambridge Journal of Economics, 38,* 153–180.

Tham, S.Y. (2003). ASEAN competitiveness in automotive. *Annual Conference of the ASEAN Economic Association*, pp. 19–21.

Tham, S. Y. (2004). Malaysia policies for the automobile sector: focus on technology transfer. In R. Brusser & Y. Sadoi (Eds.), *Product network in Asia and Europe.* Routledge Curzon: London.

Tham, S. Y. (2014). Trade policy formulation in Malaysia: Navigating between the economic and race paradigms. In A. Milner, A. R. Embong, & S. Y. Tham (Eds.), *Transforming Malaysia dominant and competing paradigms.* Cambridge University Press.

Tham, S. Y. (2015). Trade liberalization and national autonomy: Malaysia's experience at the multilateral and bilateral levels. In J. M. Nelson, J. Meerman, & A. R. Embong (Eds.), *Globalisation and national autonomy: The experience of Malaysia.* Singapore: Institute of Southeast Asian Studies (ISEAS).

The Report. (2008). Malaysia 2008 Oxford Business Group.

The Star. (2009). PM announces slew of liberalization measures.

The Star. (2012). Proton denies MD has quit. https://www.pressreader.com/malaysia/the-star-malaysia/20120411/282591669924326.

Thoburn, J. T. (1973). Exports and the Malaysian engineering industry: A case study of backward linkage. *Oxford Bulletin of Economics and Statistics, 35*(2), 91–117.

Torri, T. (1991). Changing the manufacturing sector, reorganizing automobile assemblers and developing the auto component industry under the new economic policy. *The Developing Economies, 29*(4), 387–413.

UNCTAD. (2006). *Trade and development report*, 2006. New York: United Nations Conference on Trade and Development.

UNCTAD. (2013). *Global value chains and development: Investment and value added trade in the global economy, a preliminary analysis.* Geneva: United Nations Conference on Trade and Development.

Wad, P. (2009). The automobile industry in Southeast Asia: Malaysia and Thailand. *Journal of the Asia Pacific Economy, 14,* 172–193.

Wad, P., & Govindaraju, C. V. G. R. (2011). Automotive industry in Malaysia: An assessment of its development. *International Journal Automotive Technology and Management, 11*(2), 152–171.

Whah, C. Y. (2012). The Evolution of Malaysia's development strategies and the global economy: Responses from SMEs and civil societies. *The Copenhagen Journal of Asian Studies, 30*(1).

World Trade Organisation (WTO). (2012). *Trade policy review.* https://docs.wto.org/dol2fe/Pages/FE_Search/FE_S_S009-DP.aspx?language=E&CatalogueIdList=122030,100985,106138,100718,55687,108108,41079&CurrentCatalogueIdIndex=0&FullTextSearch.

Chapter 4
The Political Economy of the National Car Project

4.1 Malaysia's National Car Project

The national car project forms a significant part of Malaysia's industrial policy. It has also suggested that the state adopted a developmentalist state approach like Northeast Asian countries (Abbott, 2003; Kanapathy & Hazri, 2013). The project became part of the country's *developmental legitimacy*, where development in the automotive form is the most important legitimising principle of the state, while the national automotive policy is characterised as *plan-rational* to promote the automotive sector by allocating resources and protecting the enterprise (Abbott, 2003, 2004). This enabled policy actors to coordinate, prioritise and mobilise resources in the policy-making institutions. The NAP has been primarily evolved around the interest of national car project. The NAP has strong adaption to the domestic political economy, and while development of the automotive industry is an important end goal, political considerations can subordinate economic goals.

Though the national car project is embedded with political interests, it is intended to strengthen the country's industrial base and promote technological innovation activities. The automobile sector is a highly capital-intensive sector that requires a substantial amount of resources to be invested in various areas such as physical infrastructures, modern technology and human capital development. Though at the outset Malaysia had a limited industrial base for the development of automotive industry, given the existing institutional capacity the political institutions able to allocate state resources attempted to shift its comparative advantage (Lall, 1995). Through early development of the national car project, Proton depended considerably on Japanese technology (in a joint-collaboration with Mitsubishi Motor Corporation), but the intention was to move up the production chain to become a full-fledged carmaker. According to Mahathir,

> ...Proton is a national interest that planned to become a homegrown Malaysian car and as part of industrialising the country with automotive sectors, so policy will move to this end...also to show the world that developing country can do it as well...

F. Suffian, *Political Economy of Malaysia's Industrial Policy*,
https://doi.org/10.1007/978-981-33-6901-6_4

To this end, Malaysia's government formulated industrial master plans to ensure the national car project can become a full-scale manufacture of motor vehicles. The formation of the national car project was the lynchpin to meet the industrial master plan of the country (Ariffin et al., 2016). The first Industrial Master Plan (IMP I 1986–1995) was introduced subsequently after the government launched the heavy industrialisation programme. IMP I emphasis was to lay the foundation of manufacturing industries, particularly non-resources based for industrial development. Technological acquisition and upgrading to enhance production, processing and value addition became a central part of industrial policy. Formation of the national car project through Proton was to lay the foundation for manufacturing activities. Collaboration between with Mitsubishi Motor Corporation and later with French car company Citroen was part of strengthening technological acquisition at the early stage. Proton Research and Development centre was set up to carry out full-scale research on computer aided engineering design, model making and manufacturing (Tham, 2004) (Fig. 4.1).

Subsequently, IMP II (1996–2006) was formulated to increase productivity and competitiveness, building upon IMP I. As such, IMP II reiterated the focus on the development of locally produced components and technological deepening this

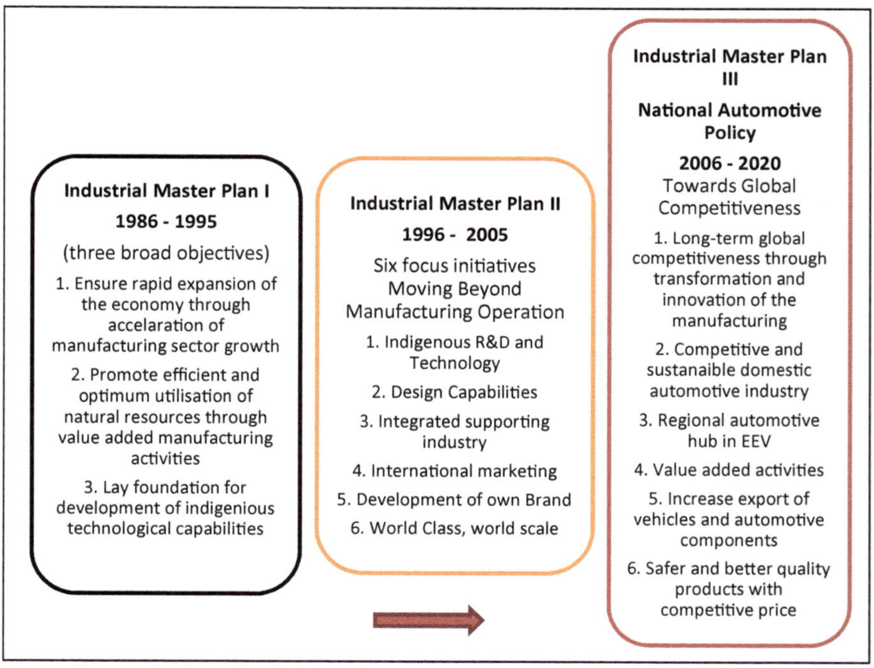

Fig. 4.1 Phases of industrial master plan and national automotive policy (*Source* Ismail, 1990; NAP, 2014, 2020; MITI, 2016)

sector. At this stage Malaysia was preparing to abolish the local content requirement, therefore the plan was to expand scale of production, upgrade technological capability, develop of human resources, and increase product and engineering capability and production process technology (Malaysia, 1996). The IMP II attempted to broaden manufacturing capabilities through the strategy of cluster-based industrial development, commonly dubbed as *manufacturing plus plus* (manufacturing + +). The development of an industrial cluster provided the state a strategic focus on selected industries, especially the national car projects, to move up the global values chain. IMP II entails more development of physical infrastructures and strengthening linkages. The cluster-based industrial development led the government to establish Proton City, Tanjung Malim, the second factory built with a production capacity of more than 500,000 for Proton. Special institutes such as the Technology & Industry Advancement Programs were established under MITI to oversee the progress of the automotive industry.

Despite the adverse economic and social costs of the 'national champion product' (the national car project). The national car companies such as Proton and Perodua have been able to manufacture and design their own cars (Govindaraju, 2010). Proton was able to do this after the company acquired British Lotus Group. With full ownership of the British car company, Proton was able to access Lotus technology to develop its own design and engine. Perodua[1] also produces and designs its own car in a lower segment of Malaysia's automotive market, though the company is strictly monitored by its partner Daihatsu, which is under Toyota's *keiretsu* (Wad, 2009). In general, both national car companies have the capacity to manufacture their cars within the existing platform, manufacturing stamping dies, plastic moulds, powertrain design, R&D and engine manufacturing which characterised as capital intensive activities.

Despite criticism levelled upon the national car company, based on the interview data most respondents agreed that if it was not for Mahathir orchestrating the implementation of the national automotive policy the country could not have gone this far. Malaysia took 'independent development' in its industrial policy in the automotive sectors, while most of Southeast Asia still retained 'dependency development' (Doner, 1992; Tai & Ku, 2013). For instance, in Thailand, Indonesia and the Philippines the domestic automotive sector is highly dependent upon Japanese companies' production network (Hatch & Yamamura, 1996; Kobayashi et al., 2015). Taking an independent development mode means the industrial policy enabled the national car company to pursue export-oriented strategy and less dependence on foreign automakers. However, the extent of the benefits of taking an independent development mode in industrial policy remains a debatable issue for a developing country like Malaysia. Though the national car resembles an independent mode of automotive production, in terms of economies of scale and technological advancement it

[1] Initially Malaysia company has majority share over Perodua, after restructuring the company in 2001 the Japaneses company—Daihatsu, hold majority shares (Rosli & Kari, 2008, p. 94). Perodua has strict application of the Japanese production standards and procedures. Basically Malaysia company mainly manages sales of the automobile.

remains limited. Most of the technology used still depends on foreign companies, including purchasing licenses (the right to use foreign technology), which reflect limited indigenous technology development (Tham, 2004; Zhang et al., 2017). This affects the competitiveness of the national car company. Competitiveness has been the problem for the national car companies, particularly Proton.

While this research will focus on the political economy of Proton, which is the only national car wholly owned by Malaysian companies, it is important to point out the nature of Perodua. Even though both are labelled as national cars there is difference between Proton and Perodua. The second national car project i.e. Perodua is established in 1993. The early formation of Perodua was a joint collaboration with Daihatsu and Mitsui and several government-controlled companies such as PNB Equity Resource Corp Sdn Bhd, Med-Bumikar Mara and UMW Corporation, where Malaysian equity amounted to 68 per cent and Japanese equity 32 per cent (Wad & Govindaraju, 2011; Rosli, 2006). The establishment of Perodua and Proton is somehow similar where both began as joint ventures with a Japanese company. Perodua was formed to further complement the Proton vendor programme, which had limited economies of scale. Having the second national car that focussed on the lower segment of the automobile market, Perodua could procure parts and components from Proton vendors without directly competing with Proton's models and market.

Based on the interview data, Perodua was not merely formed to expand the vendor development programme, but the government also intended to pressure Mitsubishi for being slow in transferring technology to Proton. There seemed to be resistance from Mitsubishi to transfer technology. Although purchasing production techniques and rebadging the Mitsubishi models was part of the learning-by-doing process, it was not the overarching intention of Proton. Technological advancement in Proton did not really occur due to limited technological transfer by Mitsubishi. Therefore, the government launched Perodua as an alternative strategy to pressure the Japanese company to improve Proton's technological capacity. At the outset, Perodua also depended on the government's protectionist measures to grow in the market. It 'freerides' the automotive policy at the time when Proton was introduced in the market with high tariff barriers, tax exemptions, financial supports and subsidies from the government. The formation of Perodua has increased the localisation programme and promoted the vendor development programme (Fujita, 1999).

In 2001, Perodua began to restructure its joint venture agreement. The new agreement saw 72 per cent Malaysian companies equity on a vehicle sales firms, while the manufacturing and engine manufacturing firms were 51 per cent controlled by Daihatsu and Mitsui. The qualitative data reveal that the second national car company has control over sales. Having a majority share of the vehicle sales, Perodua retains its national car status and remains a beneficiary of the National Automotive Policy (NAP). Based on the terms of policy in NAP that intended to support the national car like Proton, Perodua also benefited from policies such as the Industrial Adjustment Fund, lower excise duties and tax exemptions.

The new structures allowed the Japanese companies to have more control over manufacturing and engine development. Manufacturing and engine development are highly capital-intensive activities and involve in R&D for engine manufacturing.

They are the central activities for car production. The Japanese have control over the manufacturing and engine development, they can employ a strict monitoring system among vendors engaged in Perodua production chains. The quality of an automobile is highly dependent on the competency of the suppliers for accessing auto parts and components. Vendors linked to Perodua tend to have joint ventures with Japanese suppliers (OEMs) and expect vendors to supply good quality auto kits (Othman & Rusop, 2007). Most vendors working closely with Japanese suppliers benefit from technological transfer and improve firms' capacity and productions. This enables vendors to produce quality parts and components for Perodua. Since the second national car is linked to the Japanese production network, Perodua is able to learn Japanese management skills, cost effective production skills and modern technology (Natsuda et al., 2013; Chrysler, 2010). The empirical evidence suggests that though the Japanese have strict control over the selection of vendors, Perodua remains in facilitation of Bumiputra vendors. There are competitive Bumiputra vendors growing out of Perodua's production chain. Having a Bumiputra vendor enables Perodua to obtain designated funds for automotive development programmes under the NAP. Furthermore, the second national car company has been able to obtain more tax reductions because Perodua procures auto parts and components from local vendors. This means the car has higher local contents, and therefore it qualifies for higher excise duties exemptions.

Even though Perodua is a national car, after the restructuring of the joint venture agreement, Daihatsu and Mitsui have more control over the manufacturing operations and R&D (Malaysia Today, 2018). This also enables technological transfer to occur and improve the firm's technological capacity. Unlike Proton, after the restructuring agreement of Perodua, the government has less interference in its management and technological development. The local vendors and Japanese company have freer arrangements for procurement of parts and components. Malaysian stakeholders can secure rents from the subsidiary of the leading automaker in the world, the Toyota Motor Corporation that controls Daihatsu (Wad & Govindaraju, 2011). By being labelled as a national car, the company retains some benefits under the NAP. As such, Perodua's competitiveness increases, which has been the reason that the second national car has expanded their domestic market and surpassed Proton. Though Perodua is more competitive than Proton, the second national car remains dependent on the domestic market similar to Proton, as Perodua has not yet to become a competitive exportable brand in the global market (Paultan, 2018).

4.2 The Politics of the National Car Project: Proton

This section will focus on Proton, which is the only national carmaker wholly owned by a Malaysian company[2] (up until 2017). Formation of the national car project had significant implications on the automotive industry. On the political front, the

[2]This research was conducted before the government recently sold Proton's 49.9 per cent share to Zhe Jiang Geely, a Chinese company who owns Volvo.

project is not just seen as modernising industrial development but is also a symbol of nationalism (Jomo, 1994). At the outset of the industrialisation process, the state took a developmental state approach through a nationalist import-substitute strategy. Since the institutions are embedded with racial consideration in economic development, the national car project is a response to the NEP objectives that aim for the creation of the Bumiputra business community and a Bumiputra labour force to lead modern sectors of Malaysia's economy, which were previously dominated by Chinese business groups (Wad & Govindaraju, 2011; Jomo, 2008; Doner, 1992). Having framed the project with nationalism, including ethnocentrism, the governing elite have used this project to come out with various policy arrangements to secure the national interest and allocate a substantial amount of resources to promote the growth of the national car project.

Though the political elite packaged the national car project with nationalist sentiment along with the need to increase participation of the Bumiputra group in the automotive sectors, there is also economic reason underlying the national car project. The purpose of the project is to rationalise the automotive industry (Abdulsomad, 1999; Doner, 1992). Prior to the heavy industrialisation programme, there were numerous foreign automotive manufacturers who produced low volume with rapidly changing models and makes. This led to market fragmentation and hindered the development of local auto kits and component producers. The rapid proliferation of models and makes has caused short-term production runs, uncertain demand and greater learning difficulty for local parts and components firms (Abdulsomad, 1999, p. 288). Economies of scale are unlikely to be achieved in a fragmented automotive market with rapidly changing demand for new parts and components. Though the local content policy was introduced foreign automakers resisted compliance with the policy due to inferior quality of parts and components. As part of the industrial development strategy, the government launched the national car project that is Proton to rationalise the automotive market. After the formation of the national car project Malaysia's government managed to reduce the number of models produced by foreign companies, thus creating a more conducive environment for the development of Malaysia's automobile industry (Doner, 1992). This is similar to the strategy employed by the South Korean government when it restricts foreign auto companies and enables Hyundai to lead the automotive sectors.

The interview data suggest that the formation of the national car project was meant to have better control over the market, rather than having no control over the domestic automotive industry. Car production absorbs large funds due to imports, and purchase of cars and components from foreign companies would involve a big outflow of funds. This may result in a trade deficit, and furthermore the country may be unable to generate enough wealth internally to pay for imports. Having the national car enabled Malaysia to limit imports, though undeniably the country still needs to trade with other countries, at least as the national car project could reduce trade deficits. The heavy industrialisation programme through automobiles was intended to address the problem of industrial dualism, foreign domination of high technology and export, while the domestic manufacturing sectors are restricted to small medium enterprises in mid or low tier functions such as assembly and subcontracting (Tan, 2014; Menon, 2008).

A pertinent question in relation to Malaysia's national car projects is asks to what extent the project has served its purpose for industrial development after more than three decades. So to what extent has the role of elites facilitated the growth of the made-in-Malaysia car? The important discussion here revolves around Proton, because it is the only national car company owned by Malaysian corporations (see Table 4.1) and it is the result of the first national car project, which intended to rationalise the Malaysian automotive industry. After the company was privatised under Mahathir's privatisation plan, it appeared to signal the 'rolling back of state.' However, the reciprocal relationship remains close between the political elite and

Table 4.1 Historical development of Proton

Period	Events
1983	1st National Car Project approved between HICOM and Mitubishi Motor Corporation (MMC)
1990	Proton converted into a public company and listed in Kuala Lumper Stock Exchange in 1992. This is due to the privatisation plan in line with Mahathir's neoliberal policy to enable private-sector as an engine of growth
1995	Khazanah (Ministry of Finance Investment Arms) sold 32% state to HICOM without open tender for an estimated RM 1.72 billion to Mega Consolidated Sdn Bhd. Then, Mega Consolidated owned by Diversified Resources Bhd (DRB), which was Yahya Ahmad's (a close friend of Mahathir Mohammad) main listed company. With the acquisition of HICOM both DRB and Mega Consolidated owned 95% of HICOM, hereafter became DRB-HICOM[a]
1996	Proton acquired 64% stake in the British company, Lotus Group International Limited
1997	Asian financial crisis caused DRB-HICOM financial difficulties and unable to pay Proton mounting debts
1998	State-controlled Petronas took over DRB-HICOM's share of Proton. Later, Khazanah (a government linked investment agency), bought the largest stake of 43% and tied to DRB-HICOM
2003	Proton became a fully private Malaysian company. The company also owned Lotus Group International Limited. Mitsubishi Motor exited as minority shareholders
2012	Khazanah divested their stake in Proton, now it is acquired fully by DRB-HICOM (new owner is Sheikh Bukhari who is close friend of Mahathir Mohammad). DRB-HICOM financial performance and share price decline significantly after taking over the Malaysian national carmaker in 2012. DRB-Hicom reported a pre-tax loss of over RM821m (close to US$200 m) in March 2016, compared with a RM502m profit in the previous year. Group revenues dropped by 11% to RM12.17 billion
2017	*Latest development, In 2017, DRB HICOM sold its stake to Zhejiang Geely through which the Chinese company acquired 49.9% share of Proton. DRB-HICOM also sold its Lotus Group stake to Geely

Source Tan (2008), Wad and Govindaraju (2011), Just-Auto (2017)
1 USD = RM3.059 (Malaysian Dollar) based on the currency 2010
[a]DRB HICOM also assembles CKDs such as Mercedez, Suzuki, Volkswagen, Audi, BMW
* Latest development of Proton

Proton. The political elite have substantial influence on the direction of the company. The main shareholders of Proton are still controlled by Bumiputra individuals. The sale of share has always gone through informal negotiations between individuals or has been based on close connection arrangements (the patron–client network) (Tan, 2008). The company has never gone through a competitive bidding (Tan, 2008; Gomez & Jomo, 1997). There are political influences to ensure that Bumiputra individuals are retained as major shareholders to meet the broad NEP objectives.

Privatisation of the national car company in the early 1990s was part of the government strategy to improve the company management and increase efficiency, profit and technological upgrading. The company managed to improve sales (on the back of the government's high tariff protection) and management efficiency. Privatising the national car company meant it had more tractable management structures and being privately owned enabled the company to have more flexibility to determine its business strategy, investment and direction. The company was also able to decide the capital investment requirement for technological acquisition. The existing reciprocal relationship between government and private enterprise enables it to devise allocation of resources and adjust terms of economic policy to allow the company to have sufficient resources to grow from their investments (Paultan, 2015). However, in the case of Proton, the benefits of privatisation such as flexibility and freedom are unlikely to occur because the role of institutions constrains the development of the company. There are strong political influences on the direction of the company, which include choices of candidates to head the enterprise (the government mainly prefers Bumiputra candidates), types of investments, technological acquisitions and selection of vendors, among others (Tan, 2008). Furthermore, the desire to promote Bumiputra participation in the auto industry has undermined the growth of the national car company, because the ecosystem of the auto industry neglects some productive producers (mainly Chinese suppliers) in the sectors (Jomo, 2007; Fleming & Soborg, 2016).

While the national car company has shown its capability to manufacture its own automobile and, by some indicators, to increase of production capacity over the years, its inability to innovate an exportable brand in a broader market outside of Malaysia indicates that there are problems in 'technological catching up'. The key competitiveness of the automotive industry is the ability to develop technological catching-up policy and graduate into higher levels in the production chain (Humphrey, 1998), enabling it to expand into the export market to improve economies of scale and scope. The main problem for Proton is technological upgrading (more discussion in the next section). In the haste of creating Proton in the phase of early industrial development, the government has failed to secure a favourable framework for technological transfer agreements with Mitsubishi and devise plans for exports. After more than a decade of joint collaborations, Proton merely 'rebadges' Mitsubishi models to sell in the domestic market, including models like Saga and Wira. Most technological transfer involves a high purchasing licensing contract with the Japanese company in order for local engineers to learn. However, learning in technological catching up seems limited because the company is unable to absorb, adopt, integrate and develop indigenous technology (Felker & Jomo, 1999; Tham, 2014; Rasiah, 2011a).

Though at the outset purchasing licences or contracting for copying machinery is important for the *learning by doing* process. Through such a process a foreign company will usually bring in different levels of technology usually the less superior ones for local firms to be transferred. To improve indigenous technology, it emphasises the absorptive capacity of the local company to upgrade the existing technology (Okada, 1984). Though Proton has benefited from learning lean management, after sales service (repairs), on-the-job training (OJT) and technical training in Japan, the problem with Proton is that it does not have the right management or engineering expertise to meet learning requirements in technological transfer. This is partly due to the ethno-coloured policy embedded in the selection of staff and the patronage appointments of heads of management. While the bureaucracy like MITI plays a role in facilitating the growth of Proton, too many political influences in the bureaucracy has led to the government agency to be less meritocratic in assisting the national car company, including in decisions on subsidies and the formation of R&D organisation. This is largely influenced by the agenda to meet the needs of Bumiputra interest. Subsidies in the form of grants are akin to economic rents, which the government continues to provide for Proton with less consideration on its performance (Jomo, 2007). Though the government has set up technical and training organisation and R&D agencies, ethnic requirements have compromised the skill development in the automotive industry (Fleming & Soborg, 2016). Rasiah (2009) also argues that there is a lack of university-firm linkages that hinders research and development progress that can potentially create positive knowledge generation in the automotive industry. This has implications on the absorptive capacity of the company. Due to lack of technical expertise causing a slowdown in technological transfer, Proton engineers opted to use existing components and make modifications to the existing body (Tan, 2008; Yin, 2016).

The existing de facto protectionist measures in the automotive industry, made through high excise duties and designated special funds for Proton against the backdrop of shrinking domestic market shares and sales, reveals that the company lacks competitiveness. This also suggests that the national car company requires more resources in terms of technological advancement. To increase efficiency and competitiveness, the company needs to improve economies of scale, scope and speed to finance R&D intensive activities. R&D is crucial to compete in the market, but the cost to finance Proton technology and capabilities is substantial for R&D, the company needing at least more than US100 million in product development (Rashid, 2006). Proton tends to get preferential access to state funds in R&D through informal institutional arrangements. Though Proton is likely to obtain support from the government, its focus on the small domestic market with limited exports does not help its scale economies and could not support the cost of R&D activities (see Table 4.2). Even to just break even, the company would be required to maintain sales at 100,000–200,000 units, which is unlikely in such current situation (The Stars, 2017). For example, the new model Proton Iriz (1.3 cc compact car) cost about US116 million (including R&D costs) and needs to sell at least 200,000 units within five years (The Star, 2017). To be economically viable, Proton has to attain at least 60 per cent of

Table 4.2 Proton's sales and exports ('000) and growth rate

Years	Unit sales ('000)	Exports ('000)	Exports growth rate %
2000	194.5	14.5	
2001	222.5	8.8	(39.3)
2002	222.9	8.2	(6.8)
2003	170	8	(8.2)
2004	177.9	17	112.5
2005	176.5	12.7	(25.29)
2006	125.1	14.7	15.74
2007	126.4	17.3	17.7
2008	160.6	17.3	0.0
2009	160	13.8	(19.8)
2010	177.7	15	8.7
2011	179.7	16.1	7.3
2012	143.6	13.3	(17.4)
2013	138.7	5.1	(61.7)
2014	115.7	4.3	(15.7)
2015	102.7	5.6	30.2
2016	76	n.a.	

Source Various sources including Tan (2008), Wad and Govindaraju (2011), Proton Annual Report (2009), The Star (2016), Livelifedrive (2014), Malaymail (2014)

the domestic market, or 353,005 units (Goh, 2015), and this still underutilises its production capacity that is designed for 500,000 units.

Since Proton is backed by the government, the company has facilitated the development of vendors in Malaysia's automotive industry. Vendor development is the key to supply quality parts and components in the automotive industry. The large number of Bumiputra vendors has grown through Proton's supply chain network. The Bumiputra vendors also integrated into the Perodua production chain. Local auto parts manufacturers like APM Automotive, Sapura, Delloyd, TCM Stamping, Ingress and Hicom Teck See Manufacturing are some of the successful vendors. These vendors produced the original equipment manufacturer (OEM) parts and components, such as stamped metal and pressed parts, plastic injection moulding and machining, not just for Proton and Perodua but also for Japanese and European car companies (MIDA, 2014, 2016).

Though there are other vendors that have moved up the values chain of automotive parts and components production, however majority of the mostly Bumiputra vendors remain uncompetitive in the automotive production chain (Rosli & Kari, 2008). Most Bumiputra vendors enjoy the patronage system in Proton and it is difficult to remove them from the network because of ethno-economic requirements to develop the automotive industry (Gomez & Premdas, 2016). Since there is a requirement

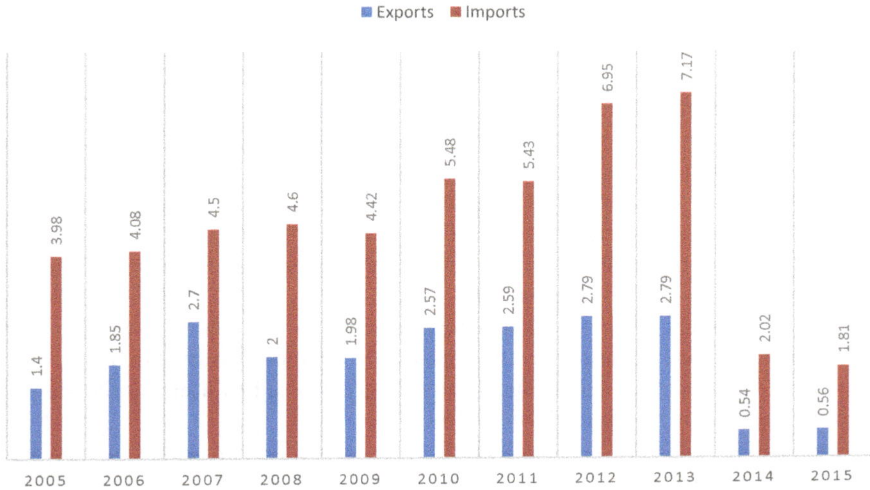

Fig. 4.2 Imports and exports of Malaysia motor vehicle components and parts (RM Billion) (*Source* MIDA, 2016)

to source from domestic vendors, particularly for the national car company, given the limited technological and production capability among Bumiputra vendors, this raises imports of motor vehicles components and parts in Malaysia's automotive industry (see Fig. 4.2). The increase of imports over the years has led to a trade deficit in balance of payment because automotive equipment depends so much on imports, particularly from other ASEAN regions where there are well-established foreign OEMs (Tham, 2004). This links back to the local content requirement as discussed in previous chapter under the NAP. Some foreign auto firms made arrangements with local vendors to import certain components in order to obtain tax reductions.

4.2.1 Technology Development

The formation of the national car projects through industrial policy was initiated to enable Proton to develop its own indigenous technology. The developmental state approach employed by South Korea to develop their automotive industry provided a certain degree of freedom for automotive companies like Hyundai/Kia to come out with strategies to acquire necessary technology that could be absorbed and integrated in the domestic automotive industry (Amsden, 2001; Weiss, 1995). The reciprocal relationship between the South Korean government and *Chaebols* negotiated plans for technological catch up. The bureaucracy played a strategic role in policy planning to guide the selected firms in heavy industrial development. Information obtained from the private enterprise through an arm's length relationship with the bureaucracy was used to plan policy that tailored the need for private enterprise to catch up and attempt to graduate into higher automotive production chains with less dependence on foreign auto companies (Amsden, 2001; Doner, 1992). The reciprocal relationship between the state and firms worked as a positive pressure for firms with a certain degree of freedom in decisions to increase their production efficiency, in order to sell their products in the export market (Amsden, 1989; Weiss, 2000). In the case of Proton, the institutional context also accentuates the reciprocal relationship between the state and firms, but companies have limited freedom to decide strategies including technological advancement (Rasiah, 1997; Rasiah and Jomo, 1999; Samsuri, 2017). The qualitative data reveals that technological development plans and even administrative matters are subject to top political leadership approval. Political interference in Proton became an institutional constraint in terms of technological development. In addition, in many instances Proton appeared to be unprofessional in its decision-making process because the political interference has led to a dictatorial style in leading the company (Awani News, 2016).

This centralised decision making on strategies of technological catch up may be a disadvantage for Proton. However, the institutional capacity that structures the power of the political elite can in some ways be an advantageous position for Proton (deemed as national interest) to acquire necessary technology, especially when acquisition of technology involves substantial costs (Rasiah, 1996). Furthermore, given the rapidly changing environment in automotive technology and liberalisation, the role of the state elite can protect the national car company. Learning is also facilitated from protective policy along with access to state resources.

Ever since the limited technological transfer problems occurred between Mitsubishi and Proton, the company (with the assistance of the government) has attempted to increase competitiveness by reducing costs, increasing production, reducing import content and pushing for technological development. The uneasy relationship between the government and Mitsubishi means the government is disillusioned at Japan's reluctance to transfer motor-vehicle technology and concerned at the rising cost of Japanese component imports (NYT, 1994). This prompted Proton to venture into new options by forming a strategic alliance with French Car companies Citroen and later Renault. Following the new collaboration, Proton purchased the Citroen AX engine, the cost being 50 per cent cheaper than the Proton Satria 1.3L (hatchback) modelled after Mitsubishi's Mirage/colt. This strategic alliance was made to upgrade the existing technology and put pressure on the Japanese company to ensure there is a proper technology transfer to Proton. After the purchase of Citroen AX, Proton Tiara 1.1 (small compact car) was introduced in 1996. However, the product was poorly conceived, lacked of quality and faced various mechanical problems. Given the rapid pace of technological development, Citroen later replaced the AX with the Saxo engine. Proton was unable to catch up with the development (Tan, 2008), hence this ended the collaboration with the French car manufacturers.

The major development of Proton was the acquisition of British Lotus Group International in 1996. Lotus Group is a British automotive company that specialises in high performance sports cars. The national car company acquired an 80 per cent stake in Lotus Group valued at £50 million. In 2003, Proton's stake increased to 100 per cent. Given the political elite's vested interest in Proton, it is unlikely that the national car company acquired the shares of Lotus Group without special arrangements using substantial government funds to purchase the stake. Yahya Ahmad, a key shareholder of Proton and close friend to Mahathir, was instrumental in purchasing Lotus Group (Reuters, 1996). An interesting point here is that Lotus Group's engineering capabilities focused on luxury sports cars, though Proton was less interested in adding a high-performance sports car to its product line. Instead, their purpose was to import the engineering talent Malaysia could not hope to produce for many years (Dauphinais & Price, 1999, p. 69). By gaining the majority of stake in the company, Proton was able to gain access to necessary technology upgrading and R&D, which was a major step in upgrading the national car company's engineering capability (Rasiah, 1997).

Proton moved to improve its engineering capabilities with Lotus engineers. Proton improved the Satria 1.8 GTi model and Perdana V6 with 'Lotus-tuning', which were quite well-received in the market. Having access to Lotus technology, the national car company managed to design its own engine named Campro. Such technological upgrading was able to lift the national car company's status to Original Equipment Manufacturing (OEM). The engine was used for Proton's first in-house designs, the Waja and Gen-2 models. The model Waja showed progress, as the company no longer designed its car based on variations of Mitsubishi's Lancer. However, it still used Mitsubishi's (Carisma) chassis (platforms) for which they bought the intellectual property rights. The Waja model increased local content up to 95 per cent. With high local content saving the company from foreign exchange outflows, it imported parts and components namely for the engine and transmission from Japan and Europe.

The Gen-2 model was rushed into production in 2004 with the Campro engine platform. The car suffered from poor design and build though, and a more pressing problem was that the engine suffered from weak torque and Proton was unable to design variable valve timing technology (Autozine, 2005). This reflects slow learning and technological upgrading. However, given the reciprocal relationship between the government and Proton, substantial resources were allocated to support the growth of the local car company. To regain their market share, Proton came out with a few other models and makes to compete in the market. The Prevé model (with Lotus technology) was one of Proton's latest designs intended to capture the global market. The car achieved a 5-Star Safety Rating from the Australasian New Car Assessment Program (ANCAP) (Motor Trader, 2013). Even with this rating, the Prevé model faced difficulty competing in the export market, particularly in the ASEAN region.

Despite the attempt to capture the automotive market, the company has been unable to regain market share in the wider domestic market and export market. This is largely linked to the lack of competitiveness of Proton cars in the automotive market. To regain consumer confidence, the government and Proton re-entered into an agreement with Mitsubishi. With the Japanese company's technical assistance, Proton launched the new Inspira model based on the Mitsubishi Lancer GT 2.0. The Inspira model is rebadging the Japanese car with minimal exterior modification and with 40 per cent local content. Proton also entered into deals with Honda to come out with the Proton Perdana Replacement Model (PRM) with little disclosure of details (Paultan, 2013). However, based on the qualitative data, the deal was aimed to improve sales of the Perdana model, which targets the above 1.8 cc market segment in which most Japanese auto companies have a strong presence. After signing the deal, Proton came out with new Perdana modelled after the Honda Accord. This agreement is another rebadging of the Accord model with slight modification that likely involved a substantial cost of purchasing agreement. The Proton-Honda collaboration enabled Proton to use the Honda Accord chassis, but the engine used in the Perdana is based on the eighth-generation Honda Accord engine, which is an outmoded version (Paultan, 2016).

Proton has also ventured into designing a Proton hybrid as part of the initiative under the NAP to encourage Energy Efficient Vehicles (EEV) and meeting the global standard in automotive energy consumption. In 2012, MITI facilitated the transfer of a RM270 million R&D grant through special arrangement with the government and Proton to develop a hybrid car. Proton formed a joint venture with the UK firm Frazer-Nash Research Ltd. The owner of Frazer-Nash, Kamal Siddiqi, is a close friend of Mahathir Mohammad, hence there was no competitive bidding in choosing the research company. Frazer-Nash received full upfront payment without one electric car being delivered (The Star, 2016). Proton was expected to sell an electric car by 2014, though it was reported that the collaboration has not produced a road worthy car because the technology used was not up to the standard (Free Malaysia Today, 2016).

Based on the qualitative interviews, Fraser-Nash is a failed project because collaboration with the company was not the best option, though MITI or even Proton have no final say in this matter. Despite this, the government has used a substantial amount of taxpayer money to finance the project. Most global auto manufacturers have geared towards an electric car or hybrid. Volkswagen has set USD10 billion for the next five years to develop an energy efficient and electric car, Toyota's development of the Prius electric model absorbed USD 1 billion for research and development, and Nissan spent USD5.6 billion for its Nissan Leaf electric concept car (Financial Times, 2013; The Independent, 2017; Reuters, 2016a). Most of these auto companies already achieved economies of scale and high volume of sales in the world market to support R&D costs for energy efficiency. Economies of scale is linked to capacity for investment in R&D and requires high capital costs to facilitate innovative activities, as even the Chinese car automakers such as like Great Wall, Shanghai Automotive Industry Corporation and Dongfeng had problems financing automotive R&D (Financial Times, 2007; Tham, 2013). The small domestic market (estimated at 700,000 units) which Proton targets in Malaysia's automotive industry is unable to arrive at economies of scale, hence it is unlikely for the national car company to be able to invest in high-tech R&D.

Most foreign automobiles comply with the EURO 5 M fuel quality standard. This requires automobile companies to design engines compatible to the EURO 5 fuel standard in order to reduce carbon emissions. The NAP stated that Malaysia is using EURO 2 M fuel quality and that gradual changes to its fuel standard will be undertaken. The qualitative data analysis reveals that Malaysia's state-owned enterprise Petronas can meet the global requirement since most imported cars already meet the fuel quality standard. However, Proton remains lagging behind in terms of its engine for exhaust emissions. While most foreign companies demand the European Emission Standard, the role of governing elites has deterred the changes of the fuel standard in meeting the needs for the Proton engine. The Interview data also suggest that upgrading the fuel to EURO 5 M involves higher costs for fuel, which will lead to public outcry. Given that the UMNO political elite have undue influence over Petronas (Reuters, 2015; Johson & Mitton, 2001), increase in fuel prices may affect the already-ailing UMNO-led BN's popularity. However, given the pressure from the auto market to export the national car abroad, only recently Proton has invested USD136 million in R&D for a new range of engines, in collaboration with British vehicle engineering firm Ricardo and sports-car manufacturing arm Lotus Group (Automotive Analysis, 2016).

Owning the majority stake of Lotus Group provided Proton access to Lotus technology and engineering, hence enabling to Proton to upscale their technological capacity. Although Proton has made some advancements in its auto technology, the national auto manufacturer has not entered the automobile technological frontier (Wad & Govindaraju, 2011; Tai & Ku, 2013). Proton still faces ongoing competitiveness problems. The qualitative interview data suggests that acquiring Lotus is not the best option because there is a mismatch between the high-performance sports car manufacturer and Proton that targets the middle and lower end market segment. This mismatch causes a problematic technological transfer to Proton. The national car company has limited freedom to decide its own technological upgrading strategy due to strong political interferences in acquiring Lotus Group. Political influences become institutional constraint for Proton even in the direction of technological planning. This is expected since the company has become so dependent on the government. Technological upgrading is progressing slowly, as reflected in Proton's engineering capacity to develop models with cutting edge technology. This is linked to the ethno-colour policy that gives priority to Bumiputra engineers with less consideration of other groups to participate, and uncompetitive vendors linked to Proton has slowed down its upscaling progress (Rasiah, 2011a). The company strategy (with government directives) to enter into deals with Japanese companies to improve its market share also reflects the upscaling problem because the indigenous technology is unable to produce competitive models in the wider market. In short, the existing institutional arrangements between Proton and the government can facilitate the growth of Proton, but also constrain the national car company by limiting its degree of freedom in deciding company strategy.

4.2.2 Partnership

An important consideration in forming partnerships or mergers is partly to benefit from economies of scale, improve cost structures, and expand new space for expansive trade. More crucially, strategic alliance is central for auto firms to take advantage of excess production capacity, access to cutting edge technology, intensive R&D activities or joint technical collaboration, and to be able respond to wider export demand at various market segments (Humphreys et al., 2000). Following the benefits of acquisition and merger, most MNCs have attempted to move into this trend. A few acquisitions and mergers in the automotive industry include Volkswagen that acquired SEAT, Skoda, Porsche, Audi, Bentley, Bugatti and Lamborghini for passenger cars (Volkswagen AG, 2011), and the Renault Nissan Alliance, a Franco-Japanese strategic partnership which controls Dacia, Datsun, Mitsubishi and Lada (Automotive News Europe, 2016a). The Groupe PSA (Peugeot Citroen) also controls Opel and Vauxhall Motors (Automotive News, 2017). The TATA group, an Indian MNCs, controls British Jaguar and Land-Rover (Daily Telegraph, 2008), while Chinese Geely Zhejiang acquired Swedish Volvo and other Chinese automobile companies such as Emgrand and Gleagle (NYT, 2010).

In the case of Malaysia, even though the national car company is a full-fledged automotive manufacturer, the lacklustre performance of the company undeniably requires forming foreign strategic partners as a viable strategy to improve its performance. The Najib's administration intends to seek partnership with other global automotive industries (MITI, 2017). Though Proton has been struggling to compete with international marques for almost four decades, this does not mean other global automotive companies are not interested in forming joint ventures or acquiring Proton. Since the ASEAN region is able to produce more than 4 million cars annually and the regional production network (supported by AFTA) provides opportunities for global companies to take advantage of less tariff barriers in automotive production (ASEAN Up, 2018), forming a strategic alliance with Proton enables foreign companies to have access to the ASEAN market. Furthermore, given that the government has invested a substantial amount of resources to build infrastructure, machinery and plants, existing R&D facilities, and marketing and distribution networks (Doner et al., 2004; The Economist, 2004), for foreign companies acquiring Proton would enable them to have access to these existing facilities for further improvement. In turn, Proton would be able to access better technology with foreign partnerships, and by improving the existing technology Proton would be better able to increase its competitiveness. This can address the company's lack of economies of scale. With technical assistance from foreign partners able to improve engineering capability, this could reduce development costs for each model produced by Proton (Reuters, 2016b).

While forming partnership is part of increasing efficiency for the national car company, it tends to respond to the demand of domestic political pressure. Though the NAP intends to seek partnership to improve the Proton, it is constrained by the institutional context. Unlike mergers or acquisitions of European and Japanese automotive companies that prioritise economic efficiency, those formed by Malaysia's national carmaker are based on nationalist ideals not commercial rationale. It is likely constrained by political considerations that override efficiency of the automotive industry (Natsuda et al., 2013; Doner & Wad, 2014; The Economist, 2004). The national car company has been framed as a national interest. The national automaker is the flagship of the country, it is the car manufacturing company that has enabled Bumiputra to lead heavy industrial development (Tham, 2014). Such a sense of nationalism, along with the need to protect Bumiputra interest (those vendors depend on the Proton supply chain), has been used as policy discourse by the political elite, and has therefore infused into the policy-making institutions (Whah & Guan, 2015; Milner et al., 2014). The embedded ethno-nationalism has become an institutional constraint in most policy arrangements between actors in devising plans for seeking foreign partnership.

Given such institutional constraint, Proton has never entered into proper strategic partnerships that resulted in foreign automakers having majority share of the national car company or a properly joint collaboration (exception in the case of Mitsubishi in the earlier stage) (Carlist, 2015). Instead, most Proton technical assistance agreements are limited to specific product sharing agreements with foreign companies (The Star, 2017). Most of the product sharing agreements are to purchase licenses to use or to copy the foreign companies' technology. Product sharing agreements such as purchase licences to share platforms or powertrain entail limited technological transfer because foreign companies will share different levels of technological quality with their partner[3] (Okada, 1984; Tham, 2004).

Searching for a strategic alliance seems inevitable in order to improve the company sales, upgrade existing technology, improve marketing capability and expand to the export market (MITI, 2017). Many companies over the past decades have shown interest in acquiring Proton (WSJ, 2004a; The Star, 2017). In 2004, the national carmaker negotiated a possible collaboration with Volkswagen AG of Germany, one of the largest auto carmakers in the world. The intention of Volkwagen to seek partnership with Proton was to enhance Proton's position in the automotive production network, while at the same time enabling Volkswagen to utilise Proton's overcapacity plant in Tanjung Malim (with a 500,000 unit production capacity) to assemble cars for export in the Southeast Asian market, where the German company has limited market share (Athukorala, 2014). The German auto giant intended to use Malaysia as the main production network due to the dominance of Japanese automakers in Thailand. On the other hand, Proton could gain access to Volkswagen's cutting-edge automotive technology, and share research and development and production strategies, in the same way the German company has turned around Czech carmaker, Skoda (Reuters, 2007a). This could improve the national carmaker's technological upgrading and market access in the automotive production network (WSJ, 2004b). However, in 2006 the Volkswagen group and the Malaysian government refused to form this strategic partnership (Reuters, 2007a). The Malaysian government ended the partnership talks because they refused to have a foreign company become the major shareholder and take over the management role of Proton.

Another European carmaker, Groupe PSA (Peugot and Citroen), also bid for partnership with the national car company. The intention of the partnership was linked to PSA's five-year plan to develop a strong presence in the Asian region and plan to sell 1 million vehicles in China and Southeast Asia by 2021 (Automotive News Europe,

[3]For instance, the agreement with Honda to use the Honda Accord's older version Accord engine to improve the Proton Perdana Model. Proton also entered into agreement with Suzuki to share the Suzuki Ertiga platform and powertrain to develop a mini MPV Proton Ertiga.

2016b). Similar to Volkswagen, Group PSA intended to use Proton's underutilised production facilities as a production and export base in Southeast Asia, while taking advantage of the regional production network in auto parts and components trade. Having a controlling stake over Proton would enable the French company to broaden access to French auto technology and its subsidiaries such as Vauxhall and Opel. PSA could also broaden market access for Proton. While there are clear potential benefits to collaboration with the French company, the government also decided not to further pursue possible collaboration due to its reluctance to cede control of Proton (Reuters, 2007b; Just-Auto, 2014).

The partnership details of the national car company are rarely available in public, though it was recently reported that there are 20 auto companies that Malaysia has negotiated with over the past decades (Just-Auto, 2016, p.32). Most partnership negotiation seems futile especially in relation to ownership of the national car company. According to Mahathir,

> Proton resembles our national pride and it is our national car... if it is sold to foreigners who become major shareholder Proton will cease to be a national car...Proton will just be producing foreign cars in Malaysia....

This statement shows how a nationalist stance prevented possible collaboration between the national car company and other global auto manufacturers. Partnership talks come to a halt when foreign companies want to become the major shareholder in Proton. However, most global automakers want more ownership, which is common because they are able to control productions and management in accordance with global auto standards, lean productions and robust continuous improvement in R&D activities (Yusuf, 2004). This includes having control over the suppliers-assembler's relationship, particularly the vendors in the supply chain in order to meet the best quality standards. In the case of Proton, political consideration hinders substantial ownership of the company because there are many Bumiputra vendors who depend on the Proton supply chain. Therefore, any foreign ownership can undermine the implementation of the ethno-nationalist policy (Athukorala, 2014).

Proton has been the main provider of employment and has improved participation of Bumiputra companies in the automotive industry. The company has generated more than 200,000 employment opportunities. In relation to this, the challenge of strategic partnership will entail foreign ownership control of Proton's direction and business strategy. This includes selection of vendors and R&D companies in Proton. Mahathir points out that,

> ...once foreign companies have controlling stake over Proton some vendors will be marginalised in the production chains. They (vendors and suppliers) will close shop... lots of workers will lose their jobs and Malaysia's engineering capacity will be reduced... Malaysia will remain a third world developing country...

This is expected if Proton is acquired by well-established auto makers in meeting a higher quality standard. Based on the qualitative interview data, strategic partnership is about improving the efficiency of the national car company even though nationalism is valued. However, there is a need to address the ailing national car company which has been draining state resources for decades. Nationalism does not mean anything if the national car is labelled as inferior quality. Some interviewees suggest foreign ownership could further improve vendors linked to Proton. A more professional decision-making environment can make companies more competitive in their productions in order to maintain their place in the supply chain. Partnership can improve the vendors' technological capacity and learning to meet the quality standard of parts and components.

4.2.3 Geely Zhejiang-Proton Partnership

In Proton's most recent development of strategic partnership agreement, the main shareholder, DRB-HICOM, with government directives, has partially divested its Proton shares to Chinese automakers Zhejiang Geely Holding. Following this foreign strategic partnership agreement, Geely will take a 49.9 per cent stake in Proton and DRB-HICOM retains a 50.1 per cent stake. This agreement also saw that DRB-HICOM divested its Lotus Group share, with Zhejiang Geely acquiring a 51 per cent majority stake in the British high-performance carmaker. From this strategic alliance, it is expected that Geely will utilise production capacity and establish a manufacturing hub for Geely right-hand drive models, while Proton will be able to access the Geely platform and technologies, particularly Volvo, since Geely controls a majority stake of the Swedish car company. This first collaboration is to design a new Proton SUV based on the Geely Boyue model. Divesting part of the share may be viable strategy to expand production for the national car company, though qualitative data analysis suggests that the Chinese company is less interested in Proton than it is keen on acquiring Lotus for technological transfer. This gives the company has both access to Volvo and British technology.

The strategic partnership agreement is done, after political tension between Prime Minister Najib and Mahathir. The political disagreement has led Mahathir quit UMNO and resign as Chairman of Proton. Most political analysts point out that this agreement is part of selling Mahathir's legacy. Even though this agreement marks a new direction for Proton, but it is still respond to domestic political pressure, particularly regarding Bumiputra interest. DRB-HICOM retains a majority share of Proton and the owner of DRB-HICOM, Syed Bukhari, is in the close circle of the Prime Minister. Therefore, Proton is not entirely sold to a foreign company, as the political elite retains influence in the national car company especially relating to Bumiputra interest and the vendors linked to Proton's production chains.

After Geely and Proton partnership agreement is signed, the first ever Proton SUV after more than three decades was launched. The first SUV known as Proton X70 is modelled along Geely Boyue which designed by former Volvo car designer. The first car production mainly involves rebadging of Proton badge and assembly some parts and components. The X70 gives new found hope for Proton to resuscitate from deteriorating sales over the years. In less than four months there are more than 5,000 unit being sold in Malaysian market. In 2019 the Proton managed to sell 26,000 units of the SUV. The newly launched SUV also being exported to Brunei, Thailand, Indonesia, Australia, Pakistan, South Africa and South America. Such success has led the Geely to utilised the Tanjung Malim car plant and to roll out first CKD in Malaysia in 2020.

The challenge for the partnership agreement is the Bumiputra vendor links to the national car production network. Though government may retain some influence over Bumiputra interest in the national car company but the degree to influence the company can change when taken over by Geely, one of the most competitive car manufacture in China. The Chinese company will somehow have decision on the selection of vendor, though there is limited information on that details, qualitative data analysis reveals that Proton's policy on local sourcing that somehow favour Bumiputra vendor may have to change to more open sourcing method. This may indicate some Bumiputra vendor may be side-lined if competing with Chinese vendors. It is important to note that scale, speed and costs matter the most for Chinese firms, so companies that are not competitive enough may not have the opportunity to engage in the national car production chain.

The Geely take over somehow may improve competitiveness among local vendors, especially Bumiputra vendors that depends heavily on Proton. Although new norms does not bode well for most Bumiputra vendors, but new partnership in Proton can help vendors to be more competitive such as expand investment on R&D, upskilling worker and improve existing technology, rather than vendors operate in a 'comfortable' environment. The partnership agreement with Geely has seen Proton sales improving as compared to five years ago (Samsuri, 2018[4]). Expansion of sales means that more vendors are required by the Proton to manufacture cars. Aftersales service also improving this will increase opportunity for local vendors, especially Bumiputra to expand businesses.

4.3 The Third National Car

After Malaysia 14th General Election in 2018, the Pakatan Harapan led by Mahathir ousted the ailing Barisan Nasional under Najid Razak leadership. Mahathir was once again appointed as Prime Minister with specific condition that he will be leading the country for two years. Thereafter will hand it over to foe-turn-friend Anwar Ibrahim. Soon after he became Prime Minister the man behind the formation of first national car project now agreed to launch the 'Third National Car'. The plan was coincided with the new NAP 2020. According to the Prime Minister the project will be different from the first national car project. While the first national car project was state-led project, the third national car will be a private initiative. The project will be headed by Malaysian company DreamEdge Sdn Bhd and technologically backed by Daihatsu Motor Co Ltd. The third national car project will work in line with NAP 2020 objectives—an automotive industry emphasis on Next Generation

[4]https://careta.my/article/proton-lets-focus-on-the-real-thing.

Vehicle, Mobility as a Service and Industrial Revolution 4.0. Investment on this car project will emphasis on autonomous vehicle, electrification, Data Analytics, Internet of Things and Artificial Intelligence (AI) and alternative fuel powertrains.

Unlike Proton, the third national car company will be led by DreamEdge, a company that claims have experience in automotive industries for more than a decade. The company has been involved in turnkey projects in new vehicle development, which involves design, prototype development and developing systems for mass production (Lim, 2019[5]). In 2012 DreamEdge has engaged in joint collaboration with Nissan and Tokyo R&D Japan. Their collaboration works specifically on motorsport-based R&D, and other automotive development services. The background of the company may have shown capability to manufacture the third national car. As much as the company is capable of making the third national car, however the company financial capability remains in questions whether or not they able invest such substantial project that involves billion ringgits at the outset.

Mahathir points out the third national car project is private initiative and no government intervention. The Prime Minister also stated that no bailout plan if the car project fails. Though this may be right in policy terms but the existing institutional arrangement in Malaysia enable the Prime Minister and the bureaucracy to come out with informal arrangement to facilitate the local company. Based on the qualitative data, RM20 million has been offered to private company to develop prototype of third national car. Though it was claimed by the government as 'financial grant' to facilitate and create an environment for the development of new national car project (The Sundaily, 2019[6]). Providing grant as catalyst is similar to developmental state approach whereby the government provide big push or in another word subsidise the new third national car. The close knit-ties between elite policy makers and selected company somehow will deliberate ways how the local company can be shielded from competition. Especially when DreamEdge just started to invest in third national car. The same informal arrangements can occur to finance and subsidise Proton.

Even though DreamEdge is seen as private enterprise has no linked with government however ownership of DreamEdge Sdn Bhd shareholders is intertwined with government interest. The largest shareholder of DreamEdge is Venturetech Sdn BHD, which is 100 per cent owned by MIGHT (Malaysia Industry Government Group for High Technology, an agency under Prime Minister Department) (Lim, 2019[7]; Pillai, 2019[8]). Such interwoven relationship will retain government interest in the third national car. Institutional arrangement will be taken place to protect the interests of the company hence again may create another uneven playing field for foreign cars.

---

[5]https://paultan.org/2019/08/09/behind-the-new-national-car-just-who-is-dreamedge/.

[6]https://www.thesundaily.my/local/med-approves-rm20m-fund-for-3rd-national-car-prototype-HB355889.

[7]https://paultan.org/2019/08/09/behind-the-new-national-car-just-who-is-dreamedge/.

[8]https://www.freemalaysiatoday.com/category/nation/2019/08/10/no-public-funds-should-be-used-in-3rd-national-car-says-wee/.

4.4 Conclusion

Industrial policy is in part a function of preferences expressed in the policy-making institutions. Institutional arrangements taking place may produce different industrialisation strategies. In the case of Malaysia's industrial policy on automotive sectors, the government chose an independent mode with the formation of the national car project to pursue its industrial development. The formation of the national car project intended to rationalise the fragmented automotive sectors, but it also holds a nationalistic stance. After the launch of Proton, configuring the national automotive policy has evolved around the interest of the national car project. Given the strategic role of the government in orchestrating the preferences of automotive policy, Malaysia's industrial policy has facilitated the growth of Proton to become a full-fledged car manufacturer.

Over the decades the growth of Proton has been backed by government supports. Despite privatisation and liberalisation in the automotive industry, the national car company remains dependent on government. As the domestic institutions accentuate a reciprocal relationship between Proton and government, the growth of the company is likely subject to the political influences. Proton has less flexibility to decide its own strategy and technological development. Although the national car company can access state preferential resources, political consideration and strong nationalism has compromised its economic reasoning. For this reason, the growth of Proton is limited because the company's strategy and direction are subject to political influences. This has implications on the technological growth of Proton, which affects the competitiveness of the company. The national car company has limited innovative capacity to produce an exportable brand in the broader market. The shrinking domestic market share also indicates that Proton is under constant competitive pressure from other non-national cars. Though there is opportunity to form partnership with other global automotive corporations as part of the company strategy to become integrated in the global auto production network, the government's reluctance to cede management control has hindered strategic alliances. In short, the institutional capacity has allowed the ruling elite to devise automotive policy to promote the growth of Proton since its infancy stage, and such capacity was crucial to promote heavy industrialisation similar to the developmentalist state approach in East Asia. However, in Malaysia, the deeply embedded political influences and the concern over the Bumiputra agenda has hindered the growth of the national car company. The development of third national car has yet known, but the existing institutional arrangement between elite policy makers and selected interest, it is likely the third national car will be protected by the government through various ways similar to Proton.

References

Abbott, J. (2003). *Developmentalism and dependency in Southeast Asia*. London: Routledge.

Abbott, J. (2004). 'Not like the rest': Differential development in Malaysia and Thailand. In L. Low (Ed.), *Developmental state: Relevancy, redundancy or reconfiguration?* New York: Nova Science Publisher.

Abdulsomad, K. (1999). Promoting industrial and technological development under contrasting industrial policies: The automotive industry in Malaysia and Thailand. In K. S. Jomo, G. Felker, & R. Rasiah (Eds.), *Industrial technology development in Malaysia: Industry and firm studies*. New York: Routledge.

Amsden, A. H. (1989). *Asia's next giant: South Korea and late industrialisation*. Oxford University Press.

Amsden, A. H. (2001). *The rise of 'the rest': Challenges to the west from late industrialising economies*. Oxford University Press.

Ariffin, A. S., Sahid, M. L. I., & Mavaak, M. (2016). Factors potentially enhancing national automotive policy goals and industry innovation. *Journal of Science, Technology and Innovation Policy, 2*(1), 10–17.

ASEAN Up. (2018). Southeast Asia automotive industry overview. https://aseanup.com/southeast-asia-automotive-industry-overview/.

Athukorala, P. C. (2014). *Industrialisation through state-MNC partnership: Lesson from Malaysia national car project* (Working Paper No. 2014/06). Arndt-Corden Department of Economics, Crawford School of Public Policy.

Automotive Analysis. (2016). *Same-day analysis: Proton unveils USD136-million investment in new engine R&D*. http://blog.ihs.com/same-day-analysis%3A-proton-unveils-usd136-mil-investment-in-new-engine-rd%2C-perodua-gains-9-yy-in-2015-global-vehicle-sales.

Automotive News. (2017). *PSA reaches deal to buy Opel from GM, wins board approval, report says*. http://www.autonews.com/article/20170303/OEM/170309913/psa-reaches-deal-to-buy-opel-from-gm-wins-board-approval-report-says.

Automotive News Europe. (2016a). *Nissan takes control of Mitsubishi with Ghosn as chairman*. http://www.autonews.com/article/20161020/COPY01/310209957/nissan-takes-control-of-mitsubishi-with-ghosn-as-chairman.

Automotive News Europe. (2016b). *PSA seeks Southeast Asia expansion with Proton bid*. http://europe.autonews.com/article/20170222/ANE/170229954/psa-seeks-southeast-asia-expansion-with-proton-bid.

Autozine. (2005). *Worst car of the year*. http://www.autozine.org/Award/Au…ards_08.htm?afsrc=1.

Awani News. (2016). *Dr Mahathir must take responsibility over Proton's failure, Rahman Dahlan says*. http://english.astroawani.com/malaysia-news/dr-mahathir-must-take-responsibility-over-protons-failure-rahman-dahlan-says-100787.

Carlist. (2015). *A look at Proton's long history of MoUs that never came to pass*. https://www.carlist.my/news/look-protons-long-history-mous-never-came-pass/14600/.

Chrysler, M. (2010). Merging Malaysia's national car companies hard to justify, analysts Say, WardsAuto. http://wardsauto.com/news-analysis/merging-malaysia-s-national-car-companies-hard-justify-analysts-say.

Daily Telegraph. (2008). *Mike Rutherford ponders Tata's takeover of Land Rover and Jaguar*. http://www.telegraph.co.uk/motoring/columnists/mike-rutherford/2751431/Car-finance-with-Mr-Money.html.

Dauphinais, G. W., & Price, C. (1999). *Straight from the CEO*. New York: Rockefeller Centre.

Doner, F. R., & Wad, P. (2014). Financial crisis and automotive industry development in Southeast Asia. *Journal of Contemporary Asia Journal of Contemporary Asia, 44*(4), 664–687.

Doner, R., Noble, G. W., & Ravenhill, J. (2004). Production network in East Asia's automobile parts industry. In S. Yusuf, M. A. Altaf, & K. Nabeshima (Eds.), *Global production networking and technological change in East Asia*. World Bank and Oxford University Press.

Doner, R. F. (1992). Limits of state strength: Toward an institutionalist view of economic development, *World Politics, 44*(3), 398–431.

Felker, G., & Jomo, K. S. (Eds.). (1999). *Technology, competitiveness and the state: Malaysia's industrial technology policies*. London: Routledge.

Financial Times. (2007). *The car market: In need of economies of scale*. https://www.ft.com/content/82d00368-7796-11dc-9de8-0000779fd2ac.

Financial Times. (2013). *Toyota's gamble on the Prius*. https://www.ft.com/content/146ad23c-7230-11e2-89fb-00144feab49a.

Fleming, D., & Soborg, H. (2016). Proton—Malaysia's national car project: Between success and failure? In A. Hansen & K. B. Nielsen (Eds.), *Cars, automobility and development in Asia: Wheel of change*. London: Routledge.

Free Malaysia Today. (2016). *Proton misadventures and the need for some tough love*. http://www.freemalaysiatoday.com/category/opinion/2016/04/05/protons-misadventures-and-the-need-for-some-tough-love/.

Fujita, M. (1999). *Industrial policies and trade liberalization: The automotive industry in Thailand and Malaysia*. APEC Study Center Institute of Developing Economies.

Goh, S. (2015). *Where went wrong in Proton, KiniBiz*. http://www.kinibiz.com/story/issues/191566/where-proton-went-wrong.html.

Gomez, E. T., & Jomo, K. S. (1997). *Malaysia's political economy: Politics, patronage and profits*. Cambridge: Cambridge University Press.

Gomez, E. T., & Premdas, R. R. (2016). *Affirmative action, ethnicity and conflict*. Routledge.

Govindaraju, C. V. G. R. (2010). *Automotive industry: Trends and reflections*. Geneva: International Labour Organisation.

Hatch, W., & Yamamura, K. (1996). *Asia in Japan's embrace: Building regional production alliance*. Cambridge: Cambridge University Press.

Humphrey, J. (1998). *Assembler-supplier relations in the auto industry: Globalization and national development*. Brighton: Institute of Development Studies, University of Sussex.

Humphrey, J., Lecler, Y., & Salerno, M. S. (2000). *Global strategies and local realities: The auto industry in emerging markets*. London: Macmillan.

Ismail, M. Y. (1990). Export competitiveness: Objective and performance of the industrial master plan. *Jurnal Ekonomi Malaysia, 21*(22), 99–118.

Johson, S., & Mitton, T. (2001). Cronyism and capital controls: Evidence from Malaysia. *Journal of Financial Economics, Elsevier, 67*(2), 351–382.

Jomo, K. S. (1994). The Proton Saga: Malaysian car, Mitsubishi gain. In K. S. Jomo (Ed.), *Japan and Malaysian development—In the shadow of the rising sun*. London: Routledge.

Jomo, K. S. (2007). Industrialisation and industrial policy in Malaysia. In K. S. Jomo (Ed.), *Malaysia industrial policy*. Singapore: NUS press.

Jomo, K. S. (2008). Proton causes Malaysia inconsistent trade policy. *Malaysiakini*.

Just-Auto. (2014). Analysis Finding a way forward for Proton. https://www.just-auto.com/analysis/finding-a-way-forward-for-proton_id147512.aspx.

Just-Auto. (2016). Time is running out for Proton—Analysis. https://www.just-auto.com/analysis/time-is-running-out-for-proton-analysis_id172304.aspx.

Just-Auto. (2017). Proton to produce first Geely-based model by 2019. https://www.just-auto.com/news/proton-to-produce-first-geely-based-model-by-2019_id177822.aspx.

Kanapathy, V., & Hazri, H. (2013). *Political dimension of a middle income trap: Challenges and opportunities for reform*. Kuala Lumpur: The Asia Foundation.

Kobayashi, H., Jin, Y. S., & Schroeder, M. (2015). ASEAN economic community and the regional automotive industry: Impact of ASEAN economic integration on two types of automotive production in Southeast Asia. *International Journal of Automotive Technology and Management, 15*(3), 268–291.

Lall, S. (1995). Malaysia: Industrial success and the role of the government. *Journal of International Development, 7*(5), 759–773.

Livelifedrive. (2014). Proton's Chairman laments lack of support from Malaysians, aims to ramp up exports. http://www.livelifedrive.com/news/protons-chairman-laments-lack-support-malaysians-aims-ramp-exports/22177.

Malaymail. (2014). Proton will review export strategy, says Mustapa. http://www.themalaymailonline.com/money/article/proton-will-review-export-strategy-says-mustapa#xqjdo8yr5i67lMqk.99

Malaysia Investment Development Authority (MIDA). (2014). Business opportunity: Malaysia' automotive industry. http://www.mida.gov.my/home/32/pages/.

Malaysia Investment Development Authority (MIDA). (2016). Business opportunity: Malaysia' automotive industry. http://www.mida.gov.my/home/32/page.

Malaysia Today. (2018). *Malaysia's national car driving into a dead end? Not many options left for Proton.* http://www.malaysia-today.net/2014/06/03/malaysias-national-car-driving-into-a-dead-end-not-many-options-left-for-proton/.

Menon, J. (2008). *Macroeconomic management amid ethnic diversity: Fifty years of Malaysian experience* (ADB Institute Discussion Paper No. 102).

Milner, A., Embong, A. R., & Tham, S. Y. (Eds.). (2014). *Transforming Malaysia dominant and competing paradigms.* Cambridge University Press.

Ministry of International Trade and Industry (MITI) Malaysia. (2016). *Approve permit.* http://www.miti.gov.my/index.php/pages/view/2096.

Ministry of International Trade and Industry (MITI) Malaysia. (2017). *Factsheet incentive for industrial adjustment fund.* http://www.recoda.com.my/wp-content/uploads/2017/11/SCORE_factsheet-incentivesforindustrialadjustment.pdf.

Motor Trader. (2013). 5 stars for Proton Preve in Australasian NCAP. http://www.motortrader.com.my/news/5-stars-for-proton-preve-in-australasian-ncap/.

National Automotive Policy (NAP). (2014). http://www.maa.org.my/pdf/NAP_2014_policy.pdf.

National Automotive Policy (NAP). (2020). https://www.miti.gov.my/index.php/pages/view/nap2020.

Natsuda, K., Segawa, N., & Thoburn, J. (2013). Globalisation and the Malaysia automotive industry: Industrial nationalism, liberalisation and the role of Japan. *Global Economic Review, 42*(2), 113–134.

New York Times (NYT). (1994). *Malaysia looks beyond Japan for car technology.* http://www.nytimes.com/1994/08/11/business/worldbusiness/11iht-malcar.html.

New York Times. (2010). *Geely of China completes acquisition of Volvo.* http://www.nytimes.com/2010/08/03/business/global/03volvo.html.

Okada, K. (Ed.). (1984). *Motor vehicle industry in Asia: Study of ancillary firm development.* Singapore University Press.

Othman, S. N., & Rusop, M. (2007). *Technology transfer and development of firm's technological capability among vendors in Malaysian automotive component industry: A case study approach.* Conference Paper.

Paultan. (2013). *Proton Perdana replacement model could use Honda Accord chassis and Petronas engine.* https://paultan.org/2013/04/24/proton-perdana-replacement-model/.

Paultan. (2015). *Proton electric car still in a prototype stage—Parliament.* https://paultan.org/2015/05/29/proton-electric-car-prototype-stage/.

Paultan. (2016). *New Proton Perdana officially launched—2.0L and 2.4L Honda engines.* https://paultan.org/2016/06/14/new-proton-perdana-launched/.

Paultan. (2018). *Perodua eyes 2-3% sales growth in 2018, parts exports.* https://paultan.org/2018/01/02/perodua-eyes-2-3-sales-growth-in-2018-parts-exports/.

Proton Annual Report. (2009). www.protontr.com/pdf/AnnualReports/2009AnnualReport.pdf.

Rashid, A. (2006). *Business response to the regional demands and opportunity: A study of Malaysian automobile industry.* Available http://citeseerx.ist.psu.edu/viewdoc/summary?doi=10.1.1.123.6990.

Rasiah, R. (1996). Institutions and innovations: Moving towards the technology frontier in Malaysia's electronics industry. *Journal of Industry Studies, 3*(2), 79–102.

Rasiah, R. (1997). Rent in Proton management. In M. Khan & K. S. Jomo (Eds.), *Rents and development*. Cambridge University Press.

Rasiah, R. (2009). Technological capabilities of automotive firms in Indonesia and Malaysia, The Earth Institute at Columbia University and the Massachusetts Institute of Technology. *Asian Economic Paper, 8*(1), 151–169.

Rasiah, R. (2011a). Industrial policy and industrialization. In R. Rasiah (Ed.), *Malaysian economy: Unfolding growth and social change*. Kuala Lumpur: Oxford University Press.

Rasiah, R. (2011b). Is Malaysia facing negative deindustrialisation? *Pacific Affairs, 84*(4).

Rasiah, R., & Jomo, K. S. (1999). Introduction. In K. S. Jomo, G. Felker, & R. Rasiah (Eds.), *Industrial technology development in Malaysia: Industry and firm studies*. New York: Routledge.

Reuters. (1996). *Lotus purchased by Proton*. http://www.sandsmuseum.com/cars/elise/information/press/press/press1996/reuter.html.

Reuters. (2007a). *Malaysia ends talks with VW, GM over Proton*. http://www.reuters.com/article/volkswagen-proton/update-3-malaysia-ends-talks-with-vw-gm-over-proton-idUSL2029907420071120.

Reuters. (2007b). *Malaysia aiming for Proton partner this month*. http://uk.reuters.com/article/proton/malaysia-aiming-for-proton-partner-this-month-idUKKLR26388620070312.

Reuters. (2015). *Malaysian Prime Minister appoints new Petronas CEO*. https://www.reuters.com/article/petronas-ceo-idAFL4N0VJ46C20150209.

Reuters. (2016a). *Race-track rivalry moves to boardroom as VW brands battle for electric car jobs*. http://www.reuters.com/article/us-volkswagen-powerstruggle/race-track-rivalry-moves-to-boardroom-as-vw-brands-battle-for-electric-car-jobs-idUSKBN13M0DI.

Reuters. (2016b). *Malaysia's Proton partner search flushes out 3 carmakers with eye on ailing firm-sources*. https://www.reuters.com/article/us-malaysia-autos-proton/malaysias-proton-partner-search-flushes-out-3-carmakers-with-eye-on-ailing-firm-sources-idUSKCN11T0A7.

Rosli, M. (2006). The automobile industry and performance of Malaysia auto production. *Journal of Economic Cooperation, 27*(1), 88–114.

Rosli, M., & Kari, F. (2008). *The comparative performance of local and foreign suppliers in the Malaysian automotive industry: The case of Proton's vendor*. Paper presented at the International Conference on Foreign Direct Investment and Technology Transfer in Asia, AEI/UM, Kuala Lumpur, Malaysia.

Samsuri, H. (2017). Tun be fair to yourself. *Utusan Online*. http://www.utusan.com.my/rencana/utama/tun-be-fair-to-yourself-1.448006.

Tai, W. P., & Ku, S. C. Y. (2013). State and industrial policy: Comparative political economic analysis of automotive industrial policies in Malaysia and Thailand. *Journal of ASEAN, 1*(1), 55–82.

Tan, J. (2008). *Privatisation in Malaysia: Regulation, rent-seeking and policy failure*. Routledge.

Tan, J. (2014). Running out of steam? Manufacturing in Malaysia. *Cambridge Journal of Economics, 38*, 153–180.

Tham, E. (2013). Stuck in first gear: Chinese car manufacturers struggle to compete with foreign brands. *China Focused Leadership and Business Analysis*. http://knowledge.ckgsb.edu.cn/2013/07/30/china/chinese-car-manufacturers-struggle-to-compete-with-foreign-brands/.

Tham, S. Y. (2004). Malaysia policies for the automobile sector: Focus on technology transfer. In R. Brusser & Y. Sadoi (Eds.), *Product network in Asia and Europe*. Routledge Curzon.

Tham, S. Y. (2014). Trade policy formulation in Malaysia: Navigating between the economic and race paradigms. In A. Milner, A. R. Embong, & S. Y. Tham (Eds.), *Transforming Malaysia dominant and competing paradigms*. Cambridge University Press.

The Economist. (2004). Proton Bomb. http://www.economist.com/node/2653701.

The Independent. (2017). *Lotus to be rescued by Chinese billionaire who bought Volvo cars*. http://www.independent.co.uk/news/business/news/lotus-takeover-chinese-billionaire-geely-holding-volvo-cars-british-sports-car-a7923671.html.

The Star. (2017). *Can Proton do it this time?* https://www.thestar.com.my/business/business-news/2017/02/11/can-proton-do-it-this-time/.

The Star. (2016). *Proton's hybrid misadventures.* https://www.nst.com.my/news/2016/04/138329/protons-hybrid-misadventures.

Volkswagen Annual Report. (2011). *Strategy.* http://annualreport2011.volkswagenag.com/servicepages/filelibrary/files/collection.php.

Wad, P. (2009). The automobile industry in Southeast Asia: Malaysia and Thailand. *Journal of the Asia Pacific Economy, 14,* 172–193.

Wad, P., & Govindaraju, C. V. G. R. (2011). Automotive industry in Malaysia: An assessment of its development. *International Journal Automotive Technology and Management, 11*(2), 152–171.

Wall Street Journal (WSJ). (2004a). *VW and Proton discuss alliance in Southeast Asia.* https://www.wsj.com/articles/SB109656917845232704.

Wall Street Journal (WSJ). (2004b). *Malaysia's Proton, VW Sign deal for partnership.* https://www.wsj.com/articles/SB109881743344856119.

Weiss, L. (1995). Governed interdependence: Rethinking the government-business relationship in East Asia. *The Pacific Review, 8*(4), 589–616.

Weiss, L. (2000). Developmental states in transition: adapting, dismantling, innovating, not 'normalizing'. *The Pacific Review, 12,* 21–55.

Whah, C. Y., & Guan, T. C. (2015). *Malaysia's protracted affirmative action policy and the evolving Bumiputra commercial and industrial community* (ISEAS Economics Working Paper).

Yin, K. W. (2016). *Do Malaysians want to see Proton go bankrupt?* https://www.malaysiakini.com/news/338231#lSQ1lXJcTZCfWyMb.99.

Yusuf, S. (2004). Competitiveness through technological advances under global production networking. In S. Yusuf, M. A. Altaf, & K. Nabeshima (Eds.), *Global production networking and technological change in East Asia.* World Bank and Oxford University Press.

Zhang, M., Rasiah, R., & Lee, K. Y. (2017). Navigating a highly protected market: China's Chery automobile in Malaysia. *Journal of Contemporary Asia, 47*(5), 774–779.

Chapter 5
Political Economy Analysis of the National Automotive Industry

5.1 Political Institutions

The political institutions are the heart of policy creation and change. The dynamic of policy formulation depends on the political actors' interactions that are influenced largely by the formal institutions and normative rules of the political institutions they are embedded in (Lowndes, 2010). However, the interaction of the political elite is subject to the balance of power between other political actors. Different institutional contexts may have distributed power unequally, which is rooted from a historical specificities and normative dimension. This can limit groups' participation to advance their interests in the policy domain or to block policy preferences. With an uneven distribution of power, the institutions structure the capacity of the political elite to come out with policy ideas, preferences and strategies (Thelen & Steinmo, 1992). Having control of the policy-making domain, the political elite can mobilise resources and influence formation of industrial policy. Often, political elite frame industrial policy with ideology that is in consonance with the norms and values embedded in the institutions in order to make the policy ideas legitimate.

In the context of Malaysia's political institutions, the long-serving coalition government, UMNO-led BN (until 2017), plays a dominant role to manufacture policy interest (Chin, 2011; Brown et al., 2004). The uneven power relations of the institutional design enable the political elite to have control over the institutional arrangements in the policy-making process, hence limiting other actors to promote their own interest (Gomez, 2016; Felker, 2015). Most respondents agreed that politicians, especially UMNO senior leaders in the country, have strong leverage in policy making. They suggest that changes in industrial policy or interpretation of preferences are based on the interests and preferences of the political elite. Interpretation often links with nationalistic sentiment and ethnic consideration as part of maintaining political legitimacy. Based on the primary data collection, it is suggested that the politician has final say in national automotive policy decisions, though their preference may not be consistent with the broad objective of economic welfare. Even

F. Suffian, *Political Economy of Malaysia's Industrial Policy*,
https://doi.org/10.1007/978-981-33-6901-6_5

though the policy was intended to open up the automotive industry, most respondents emphasise that the government has done very little to liberalise the domestic automotive industry. This is clearly linked to the government interest in the national car projects as a source of national pride. The government have used this narrative to preserve the industry under national interest and retains protective measures whether directly or indirectly to support the national car project.

5.1.1 The Elite Agenda Preserving National Interest

It was Mahathir Mohammad's vision to diversify the industrial structures through the national car projects. The projects are akin to national interest. Any pro-market reforms that undermine the national interest have been hindered by the government. The qualitative data findings indicate that the long-serving ruling coalitions have constrained changes in the NAP. Though there have been changes in the NAP, liberalisation of the domestic automotive market has been gradual and limited. According to Mahathir

> *...we can have an open market* in the *automotive industry, but don't be tricked by liberalisation, we have to protect our national interest, the national car is our national interest...all countries protect their industries for various reasons, not to mention Japan, Korea and Taiwan, they also have their ways to protect their interest through certain policy directly or indirectly...*

Undermining the national car projects is considered threatening to national interest, which has been one of the important factors in driving industrial development. Though the government agreed to embrace a liberal market-based approach in the auto industry, but most respondents suggest that the government will always find ways to support the industry because the political elite control the policy agenda.

The political elite can manufacture policy interest because the national automotive industry is politically captured, and in turn the elites can use their political power to preserve their interest in the policy. The national automotive policy (NAP) agenda has been captured by the political elite. To a large extent, policy interests in the NAP have been manufactured by the political elite, particularly by Mahathir (even though he is no longer in office, as a Chairman of Proton[1] the former statesman has strong political clout in the automotive agenda). Though the main objective of the NAP is to liberalise and enhance competitiveness in the domestic automotive industry (MITI, 2014), the presence of the national car project in the domestic market may not make it easy for policy makers to adopt a wholesale liberalisation project. Protecting the national carmaker seems necessary because the company depends upon the domestic market. Also, the local automakers remain behind in terms of quality due to the problems of

[1]Recently, Mahathir has resigned the chairman position, after political tension between himself and the current Prime Minister Najib. Mahathir quit UMNO and formed a new political party, the Malaysian United Indigenous Party.

technological upscaling in the company. Lack of economies of scale causes limited R&D activities, which leads to lack of innovation in the production.

Though liberalisation is key for the national car company to be competitive in the market, qualitative data findings suggest that the government will continue to protect the national car. This is linked to the historical development of the national car projects that hindered policy changes. When the project was introduced in 1985, the UMNO leader at that time, Mahathir Mohammad, envisioned that the national car project would improve industrial development and build deep linkages. This is because car manufacturing activity involves a complex level of production processes, promotes technological advancement and vendor developments, and generates employment. The project was part of Mahathir's strategy to create industrial nationalism, but it goes beyond economic objectives, as the overarching purpose of the national car project is enabling the domestic auto firms to lead car manufacturing and more importantly, enable the industry to be led by Bumiputra groups. In other words, Mahathir hijacked the symbol of nationalism that is the national car project with ethnocentrism in order to achieve developmental outcomes.

The interview with former Member of Parliament, bureaucrats and experts from a research institute reiterate the same claims and further argues that the national car project under heavy industrialisation consolidated UMNO leadership by distributing economic rents to Bumiputra business groups, hence the national car project represents UMNO legitimacy. It is through UMNO that Bumiputra groups are able to lead the country's industrial development (Chin, 2015). When economic policy planning is beyond economic reason it is important to recognise that development strategies have been central to the political regime's legitimation, and specifically to the maintenance of the hegemony of UMNO as the dominant party (Felker, 2015, p. 140). The past decision for having national car project and creating Bumiputra industrialist groups have impacted the institutions to structure policy options with regards to the national automotive policy. Changes to the NAP tend to be limited due to the perceived 'national interest' and Bumiputra interest, as Hall and Taylor (1996) and Hattam (1993) argue that 'history matters' in constraining actor's interactions in policy arrangements. The underlying institutional structures thus restrict the set of policy ideas for change.

Due to the historical development of the national car project under the heavy industrialisation programme, the elite policy maker is constrained by the options embedded in the institutions to introduce change because the historical narrative on the national car project is perceived as national interest. Interview with senior member of parliament and who was a former deputy prime minister states that,

> *...the moment you introduced a big project like Proton and you don't know the feasibility of the project, plus it requires so many resources to finance the project...the life of Proton will depend so much on the government, especially because we know this car industry at that time is a sunset industry...so they (Proton) will not stop depending on the government, plus Bumiputra business groups depend so much on this project.*

The national car projects represent the ability of the government to manufacture its own automobile led by Bumiputra groups. The formation of local automakers has made Malaysia the only Southeast Asian country able to produce and design its own made-in-Malaysia car. Mahathir notes that *'we are the only developing country able to make our own car'*; hence the national interest is a source of national pride. This has been infused in the policy-making institutions, and policy adjustments to any pro-market reforms are likely to have special arrangements to protect the national car producers.

5.1.2 Protracted Bumiputra Agenda in Automotive Policy

In the context of the automotive policy, the Prime Minister's Office has strong leverage in the policy-making process. The configuration of policy preferences to form a local automaker reflects the political elite's interest. This is common in a state that adopts a developmentalist state approach, where the executive branch has to come out with a development vision to improve industrial development (Moon & Prasad, 1994). The institutional design enables political actors to fend off other political actor's interests, which can undermine the political elite interest. According to Mahathir,

> *when I was the Prime Minister I really wanted to industrialise Malaysia and to do so we needed knowledge, skills and capability to produce and design things...I believe the automotive business can provide this opportunity to our local manufacturers, especially Bumiputra. This may seem ambitious, as a lot of people think we are a developing country, we don't have skills, resources, Malays are stupid and so forth, but I don't want to believe that because we can make a change. This is the reason why I introduced the heavy industrialisation programme and the automotive is one of the sectors I emphasised. Of course, a lot of people disagreed with me when I wanted to introduce Proton but as Prime Minister I have leverage and authority to introduce policy. I used that opportunity and I believe in what I do...Look, I am a medical doctor by background, when I make a decision I will examine all the problem of the illness, like performing diagnosis after identifying everything, then I will come out with the treatment...so when you want to cure a cancer disease you have to remove the cancer cells, it is the same in politics, if you want to do something you have to remove those inhibiting factors in the system in order to implement a policy.*

This statement shows that the political elite espouses a developmentalist state approach where elites envision industrialising the country and playing a strategic role in policy processes to attain the developmental goal. Based on Mahathir's statement, it is acknowledged that there were objections to his policy interest by other political actors; however, in order to have his policy accepted it can be argued that the he, as the President of the political party could displace those who were against his vision. There are many instances of his Deputy Prime Minister being forced to resign due to opposing Mahathir's views (Case, 2012). Such executive dominance can fend off opposing political actors or groups, which makes configuration of policy preference based on the elite. This centralises the policy-making process in the Prime Minister Office.

The qualitative data suggest that purpose of industrial development is part of the strategy to increase Bumiputra participation in heavy industry. Linking race with economic development is an important discourse for Malaysia's policy-making process to be accepted in the public domain. As the role of institutions shape interpretation for possible courses of action (Campbell, 1997a), so 'packaging Bumiputra interest' along with the national car project is a strategy of the political elite to respond to the acceptable norms of the institutional context to pursue industrial development. Since there are a limited number of Bumiputra groups participating in heavy industrial activity, incorporating their interest is seen as crucial for political actors to increase their participation. Interpreting industrial policy with ethnic sentiment enables to convince the public about the importance of the project (Tham, 2014), including obtaining support from the right wing UMNO groups. In this way the 'interpretive frame' within the institutional context enables the ruling elite to prioritise their preferences despite there being dissenting views. Incorporating Bumiputra interest has been an accepted convention in policy configuration, including in the national automotive policy. The racial aspect has become common in policy-making discourse since the formation of the NEP. The NEP has changed the 'rules of game' in the political institutions, where the state is likely to take the role of facilitating Bumiputra in the mainstream of economic development. Such changes form path dependence[2], as political actors have vested substantial interest in Bumiputra development, making it difficult to reverse the policy. The overarching purpose of forming the national car project is for the development of Bumiputra groups in the car manufacturing industry, as Mahathir states that,

> *...the national car project is always associated with Bumiputra development. The government gives Proton to Bumiputra to handle because without Proton most Bumiputra will remain doing paperwork...they may be an engineer, a qualified one, but they will just stay in the office, they will not get their hands dirty and learn new skills. With this company, the majority of the workers are Bumiputra, the purpose being we want to convince Bumiputra they also can do work just like others in developed countries. If you don't give them this chance through Proton, then they will always work for others and they will believe that they can't do it.*

The national automotive policy has a 'locked-in'[3] effect with the Bumiputra agenda: since institutions structure policy choices, the political elite could not ignore the Bumiputra agenda in policy making. It is inevitable for race and economic interests to encompass Malaysia's policy-making institutions (Milner et al., 2014). A voluminous amount of literature highlights that the Bumiputra agenda is no longer relevant because it hinders significant policy changes to promote competitiveness. Gomez and Premdas (2016) frame it as 'institutional decline,' as affirmative action like the ethno-economic agenda leads to poor and unmeritocratic quality policy making. Furthermore, it has been the interpretative frame for most industrial policy, representing the UMNO-led BN's legitimacy to stay in power. It is also the source of the patronage system embedded in policy making that can potentially hinder

---

[2]Institutional arrangements made by actors in the past that can potentially affect outcomes at a later time (Pierson, 1993). Once path dependence exists, it is difficult for political actors to reverse the decision because they have created vast interest in a particular policy and will fight to maintain those interests (Dobbin, 2004).

[3]North (1990) describes the term akin to path dependency. What has been decided in the past may have unexpectedly long-term and inefficient consequences.

policy changes. While most respondents agreed that the Bumiputra agenda needs to be reassessed in economic policy-making, some respondents contend that the protracted Bumiputra policy remains valid and necessary. They generally agreed that Bumiputra policy is relevant to facilitate those group who are left behind in the economic activities.

Though there are pro-market reforms in the automotive industry in Malaysia, given the need to meet the Bumiputra policy in automotive industry, the government continues to play an active role to provide preferential access to Bumiputra groups. This hinders the growth of the competitive automotive market environment. However, the national automotive policy retains the Bumiputra agenda as an important objective to facilitate the growth of this group in the value chain of the automotive industry. Qualitative interview suggests that NAP still emphasis on Bumiputra agenda because there is only a 33 percent of Bumiputra contribution in the automotive industry. Hence it is the agenda still relevant to facilitate such group especially in vendor development.

Pro-market reform in domestic automotive industries is constrained by Bumiputra policy. This embedded convention has a significant ideology for political elites to interpret the national automotive policy. Policy making in Malaysia is unable to detach from the Bumiputra policy, especially under such a long-serving ruling coalition. Since the NEP was introduced in the 1970s the ruling coalition began to incorporate the Bumiputra interest in economic policy; hence, the historical economic development in Malaysia is likely to relate with identification of race in the current configuration of economic policy. Bumiputra policy becomes precedent in government policy, including in the national automotive industry. Due to the early policy discourse focused on allowing the Bumiputra to lead heavy industrialisation, to date the national automotive policy remains ingrained in the indigenous group's interest ever since the made-in-Malaysia car was introduced.

Former member of parliament of UMNO added that 'everything is *Bumiputranise*'. In general, most of the respondents agreed that the affirmative action policy has been taken for granted in policy-making process. It is also framed by elites as a way to preserve the national car company and the vendor links to the company. In many partnership agreements between Proton and foreign auto companies such as Volkwagen, negotiations tend to come to a halt because the government refuses to drop the Bumiputra policy in vendor selections.

5.2 Government-Private Relationships

Typically in a developmentalist state approach, the state takes the developmental functions and leads industrial development (Abott, 2004). The state devises a strategic economic plan setting substantive socio-economic goals and structures domestic industry with the intention to improve national economic growth. In such economies the state does not downplay the role of the market to improve domestic economy, but market entry is structured to enable the domestic firms to grow. Though firms depend on the market to grow, the role of institutions facilitates reciprocal relations between the government and selected private enterprises. Malaysia's industrial policy is to promote indigenous firms to grow (Abott, 2004; Jomo, 2004). The government will facilitate the 'selected few' private enterprises in the marketplace to meet the industrial development preferences. The existing institutional design that enables reciprocal relationships allows government and business enterprises to engage in institutional arrangements to devise policy, allowing the firms to have preferential access to state resources.

In a typical developmental state approach, the government collaborates with existing private enterprise by specifying a developmental target and forming institutional arrangements for selected enterprises to have access to state resources. The reciprocal relationship clearly aims to improve industrial development with less political considerations (Jomo, 2004; Abbott, 2003). In the context of Malaysia, collaboration between government-private enterprise is embedded with political objectives. During the implementation of the heavy industrial programme and followed by the privatisation programme, Mahathir's intention was to create a Bumiputra commercial and industrial class to lead the country's national automotive industry. Based on the qualitative interview data suggests that though there are well-established existing companies linked to the automotive production network including Boon Siew, Oriental and Tan Chong Nissan, they were not incorporated into the ancillary firms for the national car projects. Proton and Perodua were established to create Bumiputra vendors though they had little presence or experience in the industry. The formation of the national car projects with the intention to create Bumiputra industrial groups formed a reciprocal relationship between government and private enterprises, and such groups are heavily reliant on state resources.

Most of the respondents revealed that close reciprocal relationships between the government and selected enterprises are crucial for the late industrialising country to form cooperation when the country started its own automotive industry. The national automotive industry required substantial resources to push the domestic firms to grow. Therefore, cooperation between the state and firms was needed to improve strategic industry. While the analysis of the interview data suggests that reciprocal relationships are important to promote the national automotive industry, most respondents reiterated that the close relationship tended to go beyond economic objectives. Certain aspects of the NAP are unable to be removed due to strong political pressures and their business allies. Based on the interview data drawn, respondents agreed that even though the national car producers and their vendors operate as private entities in the market, the deeply embedded patronage system makes it easier for the government and the local auto firms to form special arrangements (usually through informal arrangement) behind closed doors to protect the firms under the rubric of national pride.

5.2.1 Patron-Client Network

One of the features in Malaysia's industrial development is based on state patronage, where political leaders play a strategic role to allocate resources and as such this gives rise to patron client network. However, patron client network should not been viewed negatively, in fact it is a form of cooperation that is likely to solve distributive issues and facilitate the exchange of resources. The market mechanism does not respond instantaneously to facilitate firms, therefore to certain extent patron-client network as a form of cooperation can help industry in the market. This is akin to the developmental state approach employed by Northeast Asia during the early state of industrialisation.

The main problem with industrial development through the automotive industry is that cooperation has turned into 'collusion', where close ties between elites and domestic auto companies attempt to ensure mutual benefits and that both interests are secured, despite the fact that policy arrangement has a significant impact on the market. The elites' interest rigs the efficiency of allocation of resources, which leads to negative implications on the overall welfare at the expense of the taxpayers. This corresponds to the Penang Institute studies (2017), which show that the NAP does not have significant impact on market liberalisation. While market liberalisation features a competitive market, in Malaysia's automotive market the consumers continue to pay higher prices for CBUs and CKDs due to the excise duties and other informal arrangements made by the government to protect the national car project that distort market competition. Most revenue obtained from the duties is channelled to finance the national car project with lack of public scrutiny.

Industrialising the country through the automotive industry has impacted the configuration of the national automotive policy, because the creation of automotive industry was not merely intended to form national pride, but it was also embedded with political intentions to create economic rents. Interview with one of the high-ranking government officials reveals that,

> *we [government] have to pay so much to finance this project and 'certain groups' associated with the project...this car project is like a moving train with limited rail... we have to keep on building it...*

Similarly, respondent from a leading think tank group, Malaysia Institute of Economic Research reiterates that,

the patron-client network is part of our culture, it is how it is in Malaysian policy making, especially in the automotive industry where most of the players in the industry are created by elites...it goes without saying: Proton and the Bumiputra vendors.

It can be argued that the patron-client network embedded in the policy-making process is part of the informal institutions that shape and constrain policy actors' interactions. The informal rules can affect how elites interpret policy outcome and provide a continuity element in policy change (Campbell, 1997b; Helmke & Levitsky, 2004). In this case, the national car project is embedded with political interests even though the local auto companies have been privatised. They continue to receive various financial support through beyond arm's length institutional arrangements.

Although the NAP seeks to create a level playing field in the marketplace, the government tends to facilitate the national car producers in many ways. Considerable funds received by Proton for over four decades is a patron-client in action. This is a reasonable point because the company has been an important source for industrialisation and Bumiputra vendor developments. The qualitative data reveals that over the years the national car producers have received more than RM14 billion in grants and other forms of assistance to maintain the company. The findings also suggest that the national car producers receive a RM200 million R&D grant annually with little known about it by the public. Recently the Prime Minister has announced another financial support for Proton in the form of a RM 1.5 billion loan. The Prime Minister has explicitly said that this financial support is not a bailout plan but 'soft loan' to support the national interest (News Straits Times, 2016). The decision to pass the loan has bypassed the parliament, as noted by some of the respondents who are members of parliaments who have disagreed with the agenda. However, the Prime Minister's Office has made the decision to pass the loan.

Respondent who represents from the local automotive sector explains that informal discussion with the minister will take place to discuss about Proton. The respondent points out that there is a need to ensure the company interest is not threatened by liberalisation, because the company provides various business opportunities in manufacturing activities. So, government support is essential. For example, the recent decision to offer the soft loan to Proton was to support the firms due to lack of economies of scales given the shrinking of the market share and debts incurred from procurement from local vendors. Respondents representing the national car companies and domestic vendor mention that the government needs to protect the people and there are so many vendors depending on Proton and Perodua. Therefore, the need for special treatment in the policy is undoubtedly important to sustain the company in the domestic automotive market.

Due to the interlocking interest between the elites and the national car company both parties tend to negotiate payable tax, and at times the national car companies (especially Proton) may not necessarily pay the actual tax that they owe. This is manoeuvred in opaque ways. However, the interview data indicate that the national car companies have paid taxes and contribute substantially to the automotive industry, such as through research and development. So far Proton has contributed RM24 billion to the government through tax. However, there is always special consideration for the national carmakers for tax exemptions. Though the local auto company has contributed to the government's coffers in some ways, Proton is protected in various direct and indirect ways, and that all the financial contributions are channelled back to the national carmakers through various grants and loans. This is one of the reasonable ways for the government to enable the local car company to continue in the automotive business, despite the fact that it compromises good business governance.

There are existing funds in the NAP that intend to facilitate the automotive industry. The extent to which the allocation of funds is transparent remains unclear given the presence of patronage systems. These funds are tailored to facilitate the national car projects and their vendors, pointing out that the Proton Vendor Association and Perodua Vendor Association are likely to obtain those funds (Segawa et al.

2016). Insights from the interview analysis reveal that those funds can be disguised as a form of subsidies, and that clearly such subsidies are intended to support the local auto company and vendors. For instance, one of the head of automotive business association claims that Proton vendors are likely to obtain more funds because of the need to upscale the current technology for Proton to obtain better quality parts and components. The national car producers like Proton have 'strict' requirements to procure local auto kits and components as imposed by the government (Abdullah et al., 2008). Though this is part of the strategy to maintain high local content, one of the main criteria in the decision to select vendors is based on equity and ownership of the vendors. Usually, local vendors that have close links with Proton will be chosen.

Some respondents imply that the patron-client network is important to support the local automotive industry because close network is essential to help local vendors attain economies of scale. Former high ranking officer in the national car company mentions that there is a need to provide opportunity to selected vendors '*so they can get loans, make investments to improve technology, learn more and improve the company profile…*' Close-ties provide flexibility for Proton and other vendors to negotiate terms and conditions of the procurement and technology requirements. Focusing on certain vendors provides more opportunity for the company to grow, because they able to engage in the ongoing business with the national car production networks. Some vendors engaged in the national car supply chain such as Ingress, Sapura, and Delloyd have improved their auto kits production over the years. The opportunity to learn and improve auto parts production through the national car supply chain enables the vendors to supply to foreign auto companies.

However, some vendors use the close ties to capture the rents generated by Proton, as the findings suggest that some of the vendors have taken advantage to get preferential access to the designated funds under the NAP. Though the economic rent is to foster learning for vendors to grow and improve productivity, there is no proper technological upgrading progress or upscaling effort (Tham, 2014). Evidence of high import intermediate and capital goods in transport and equipment shows the vendors remain heavily reliant on imported parts and components. Furthermore, the poor quality of the national carmakers, especially Proton, are linked to the vendors who are incapable of moving up the automotive production chains, even though these vendors have captured the rents through informal ties in Proton's vendor selection process.

The patron-client network appears to be a pervasive practice in automotive policy arrangements. The reason this network is deeply embedded in the institutional arrangements is due to the Bumiputra agenda. Most respondents stress that this ethnic-coloured policy impacts the policy configuration of the NAP. According to one of the Minister in Prime Minister Department, the Bumiputra agenda has made the automotive industry illiberal and has led to poor automotive development. As stated earlier, the Bumiputra agenda has a locked-in effect in the policy-making process, and the national car projects are associated with the growth of the Bumiputra community in manufacturing activities. The automotive policy agenda is linked to create a 'selected few Bumiputra', which is dubbed as the Bumiputra Commercial and Industrial Community (BCIC). Policy-making thus tends to create economic rents for certain Bumiputra groups but not all, because the main beneficiaries are usually those Bumiputra who have close connections with political elites.

The ethno-economic policy has detrimental effect in policy making because it creates room for patronage. So, though the automotive industry is said to have adopted open market competition, because of the Bumiputra agenda the government continues the ongoing supports for the national car project and its vendors. Interview with Professor Gomez suggests that patronage system in Malaysia has deteriorated the quality of policy-making institutions. The primary reason for this is that the patronage system, coloured by race, has been captured by the political elite to maintain their preferences in the policy.

Navigating between economic policy and the race paradigm becomes more complex because of the emergence of rent seeker demands for protections at the same time the trade policy commitment was made by the government requiring pro-market reforms (Tham, 2014). The Approve Permits (AP) are one of the contentious policies in the NAP that the government has been unable to do away with. Since the NAP was introduced in 2006, there has been an attempt to abolish the policy but efforts to do so seem futile. While the government scheduled AP to be removed in 2010, the policy was continued until 2015, and the most recent revision of the NAP stated that the government would continue the AP system until 2017. An AP is a license issued by the government to individuals to sell imported CBUs with no local contents. AP is akin to the import quota and the permits are often given to Bumiputra.

AP is an unproductive rent because it does not nurture learning in manufacturing activities (Tham, 2014; Tan, 2015). The permit only creates rent-seeking Bumiputra entrepreneurs who engage automotive trading in a protected market. The AP system has distorted the domestic automotive market. Various attempts by the foreign auto companies (for example Toyota), along with other business associations such as the Malaysia Automotive Association and the Malaysia International Chamber of Commerce, have demanded changes to the existing AP system. The permit does not provide a level playing field for foreign auto companies because the AP holders obtain lucrative custom tax exemptions. According to one of the head of Japanese automotive company,

> *An AP holder can bring in a luxury car with full specifications 40% cheaper as compared to a new car. The AP holder also pays less custom tax as compared to the franchise companies like us, which have to pay more excise duty…surely the customer will choose from AP vendors.*

AP has been instrumental in giving rise to Bumiputra entrepreneurs. The NAZA Motors, a successful Bumiputra entrepreneur who has used the AP system to grow their business. The founder of NAZA Motors, the late Tan Sri S M Nasimuddin S M Amin, has a close connection with UMNO leaders and has been identified as the largest AP holder that is non-transferrable and non-restrictive, which thus used the AP to import any brand of car (Lim, 2005). Mahathir's son is also one of the AP holders able to import the luxury sport car Porsche to Malaysia (though he sold to Sime Darby in 2010) (The Star, 2010). Major recipients of the APs, such as Syed Azman Syed Ibrahim, Mohd. Haniff Abd Aziz and Azzuddin Ahmad, collectively received 15,759 APs. These individuals have close connections with Rafidah Aziz, who was then Minister for MITI (1987–2008) (The Sun Daily, 2016). However, some AP holders have misused permits for self-enriching purposes. The AP permit can cost at average RM30,000 per permit because the right to import CBUs can generate high income in the protected automotive market of Malaysia, so demand to obtain the AP permits is competitive. It is reported that there are some AP holders who sold their permit to get quick money.

The AP system is difficult to remove due to political patronage. One of the senior member of parliament mentions that '*most AP holders are UMNO members and others who are closely connected to UMNO elites*'. Some non-Bumiputra also benefited from AP by having joint ventures with Bumiputra individuals. Given that UMNO elites have a dominant role in the policy-making process, APs are part of economic rents that can be a windfall gain for recipients who obtains the permit quota; therefore, this reinforces political patronage in the policy-making institutions (Tan, 2015). The political patronage is to secure political base support for the elites who have control over the permit quota, not only of the Bumiputra business community but also of other politically linked individuals. This was revealed as most of the respondents suggest that AP holders are the main political financier during election times and have strong political clout. Furthermore, most politicians buy cars from AP holders who offer a cheaper price than the market, so it is difficult to deal with the AP holder groups of producers who have strong political connections with UMNO leaders. It is obvious that the government is unable to remove the AP system because the patronage system is embedded with racial lines. It is difficult to initiate policy change in the NAP because the AP system can potentially undermine the ties between elites and AP holders.

5.2.2 Unusual Policy Arrangement

Pro-market reforms in Malaysia's domestic automotive industry are an inevitable phenomenon. The state commitments to liberalise the automotive industry under the AFTA and WTO show that the country is obliged to support a market-based economy to promote a business-friendly environment. Although progressive liberalisation of the domestic automotive market has taken place since 2006, elites' vested interests in the national car projects have prompted policy makers to come out with unusual policy arrangements to secure the national interest. Most respondents reveal that there are various unusual arrangements made by policy makers to secure the interest of the national car projects and other interests linked to the elites. This creates an unequal playing field environment in the domestic automotive market.

Given the strategic role of the elites in the policy-making domain, institutional arrangements among the political elite and local car manufacturers have taken place to determine prices in the market. To this end, a price mechanism is used to set higher prices for imported CBUs to protect the national cars. Car prices in Malaysia are determined by the government under a 'gazetted price' mechanism which is little known by the public. In general, setting up prices for imported cars is allowable under the WTO members' government (WTO, 2017). Each make and model of CBUs is subject to custom valuation, which is calculated based on an invoice price that includes the cost, insurance and freight charges (CIF) (Custom Act, 1967), after which the CIF will add on import duty (MFN is 30 per cent while AFTA is 0 per cent), excise duty (depending on engine capacity) and finally sales tax (10 per cent).

Under the provision of WTO custom valuation, it is required to be done in a transparent manner, meaning there should be a clear custom valuation for each make, model and trim, though the extent to which this is done in Malaysia remains opaque (Paultan, 2006). The government can influence the price of a car through 'docket price', which is the price custom values of the car companies bring in and applying the designated excise duties rather than following the value state on the invoice (Penang Research Institute, 2017). How the government determine the docket price remains unclear. Since the government can influence car prices, some companies can obtain lower 'docket price', for instance, recently Mazda was able to obtain a 'docket price' reduction to sell their car in the market. Certain foreign companies are given lower 'docket prices' and some incentives (like tax breaks) because they offer value added activities in the automotive sector such as research and development and vendor development in Malaysia (Paultan, 2014).

This research was unable to obtain further details on how custom valuation is done in Malaysia due to the sensitivity of the information; however, setting up the price mechanism is part of the institutional arrangements made by the policy elite to protect the domestic automotive market. The reason to come out with a 'docket price' for certain foreign cars is because the cost of production for Proton and Perodua is relatively high as compared to well-established foreign car manufacturers like Toyota and Honda. The obvious reason for this is that the national car producers, especially Proton, are unable to attain economies of scale. Proton has a 350,000 production capacity but the company annual sales rarely surpass 200,000 units per annum. Due to this low sale volume, Proton struggles to attain cost efficiency.

Besides using opaque customs valuations to inflate foreign cars, the government also determines car prices for certain models. This policy arrangement takes place in the national economic council, which is the highest body of the economic policy decisions in the country. Imported CBUs or CKDs with an engine capacity of 1800 cc must be sold above RM150,000 in the market. Given the non-national cars (Honda and Toyota) are more competitive and the cost of production is lower than the national car, B1 states that in a level playing field environment, the non-national cars can easily drive out the national car in the market without price setting. As such, determining prices is intended to mitigate threats to the national cars in the marketplace. Such practices are clearly inconsistent with the WTO anti-competition principle that is fair competition. Based on the principle of national treatments, imported vehicles and locally produced vehicles should be treated equally, though setting higher prices for imported CBUs and CKDs violates this principle. However, there is no complaint being lodged by foreign automakers. On contrary, such policy arrangements the foreign automakers benefit in Malaysia's automotive market because determining prices for certain models resulted in an increase in non-national car profit margins. Although the price is higher for non-national cars (especially Japanese cars), due the 'aspirational value' consumers with a higher purchasing power are willing to pay more for non-national cars (livelifedrive, 2013).

Customised incentives under the NAP are among other ways for the government to encourage foreign auto companies to build linkages for local vendors in the automotive supply chain. Auto companies procure from local vendors benefit from excise duty reductions based on values of the local content. Customised incentive under the NAP is not transparent and most automakers are unsure of the actual exemption given by the government. In comparing Thailand's customised incentive and Malaysia, Thailand has made clear provision of incentives for foreign automakers. For example, under the Thai Eco Car Policy, auto companies that procure auto kits and parts from local firms are qualified to obtain an excise tax reduction to 17 percent (down from 30 percent) and an eight-year tax holiday. In contrast, under the NAP customised incentives refer to various tax breaks, soft loans and R&D for car companies who buy from local vendors. Though the policy states there are incentives for Energy Efficient Vehicles (EEV),[4] but the extent to which companies can obtain actual exemption for EEV incentives remains unclear. Based on the interview data there are unusual arrangements by policy makers for auto companies to qualify for customised incentives. The foreign automakers are eligible for the customised incentives. Since there is unclear information about the incentive, to qualify for it 'special negotiations' will be place between the MITI and the companies. Different provision of incentives is given to different auto companies depending on the negotiations. Respondents claim that there is lack of transparency in the terms of conditions for the incentives, which leaves room for discretion among policy makers to come out with conditions for incentives.

An interesting point suggested by the respondents is that customised incentives to reduce excise duty usually requires procuring auto kits from the local vendors. The selection of local vendors is usually determined by the federal agencies, in this case the Ministry of Finance. There are lists of 'selected local vendors' suggested by the federal agencies to obtain customised incentives for excise duties reductions. The findings suggest that this unusual arrangement is made to facilitate the local vendors (not all local vendors but those who have good links with senior officials in the Ministry). It is clear that when the company increases local contents more incentive will be given. However, sometimes there are parts that are not available in the country, and some companies will arrange with local vendors to import the parts then supply the part back to the OEMs. There is no strict enforcement or monitoring process from the Ministry, so such arrangements can be easily made for foreign and local companies. This is an easy way to get tax break incentives from the government.

[4]The NAP states that EEV are defined as vehicles that meet a set of specifications in terms of carbon emission levels. This includes fuel efficient internal combustion engine hybrid, electric vehicles, and alternative-fuelled vehicles such as Compressed Natural Gas (CNG), Liquefied Petroluem Gas (LPG), Biodiesel, Ethanol, Hydrogen and fuel cell (NAP, 2016, p. 7).

5.3 Bureaucracy

Variations of institutions may not resemble the ideal type of bureaucracy in a developmental state. Historical roots can have implications on the institutional design thus affecting how bureaucracy functions. In the case of Malaysia, most respondents agreed that the bureaucracy has a considerable role in industrial policy planning and implementation, though their influence on automotive policy is somehow limited. This is due to the institutional constraints given based on the wider political influences and consideration for 'selected' business groups (usually Bumiputra groups). The bureaucracy is insulated by political institutions, but industrial policy is guided by political elites along with industrial groups linked to the elites. Strong political interventions on the terms of policy mean bureaucrats need to meet the interest of the elite. Configuration is often against the overall economic objectives, however most public officials will still find ways to assert the political elite interest in policy configuration. Most public officials will work along the political elite ideas in relation to the NAP because freedom to advise on the matter is limited. Though at times the bureaucracy was tasked with improving strategy on the NAP, the decision to change the terms of policy remains in the hands of the political elite. Political interference compromises the bureaucratic autonomy in planning and implementing the NAP. The bureaucracies are guided by political interest so most policy is often subject to policy *layering* (when new rules are introduced but do not displace the old rules) and '*conversion*' (when rules formally remain but are interpreted and enacted differently) of rules (Mahoney & Thelen, 2010).

5.3.1 Politico—Bureaucratic Ties

Based on the interview data analysis, most bureaucrats agreed that they are tasked with devising industrial policy and making feasible plans. The principle agencies responsible for industrial policy planning such as the Economic Planning Units, Ministry of Industry and International Trade, and Malaysia Industrial Development Authority devise plans, negotiate policy terms with stakeholders, and conduct R&D to improve policy. Although top public officials may have freedom in policy planning, they are always constrained by strong political considerations. Majority of the high-ranking officials at the ministries concur that the bureaucrats face tough decision in policy planning and considering political interest. Though their role is to design industrial policy based on economic interest through various consultations and studies, however economic interest tends to intertwine with political interest. At times policy may not necessarily work on the best interest of the economy, though most bureaucrats voice their dissenting views on such matter but once the Prime Minister has given his 'political inspiration' along with economic interest most key senior officials will work along with the political master's interests. Most top bureaucrats will accommodate political interest in industrial policy planning.

Bureaucratic power in contemporary Malaysian bureaucracy is derived from the political master (Beeson, 2000). Though the bureaucracies are not influenced by the electorate's decisions, the long-serving UMNO-led BN that dominates the political institutions can assert strong influences on the bureaucracy. This forms an unequal power relation between the state bureaucrats and the political elite, which constitutes an institutional constraint for bureaucrats to function independently. The qualitative data reveals that the limited role of the state bureaucracy started when Prime Minister Mahathir Mohammad introduced the heavy industrialisation programme to facilitate the growth of national car project. According to Mahathir,

> *...the policy I introduced such as the Heavy Industrialisation Programme, Look East Policy, Malaysia Incorporation (Malaysia Inc.), privatisation and Vision 2020, are all about industrialising the country. To do so, of course we have to make our government administration effective enough to support a good business environment. So, we need to reform our bureaucracy so they are effective...*

Most respondents reveal that since Mahathir, administrative reforms have changed the role of bureaucracy in economic policy making. The ideal role of bureaucracy in a developmentalist state approach is for the political elite to provide vision for industrial development, while most of the planning and implementation are done by the technocrats. However, while Mahathir attempted to make the bureaucracy effective to implement his bold plans, he has in fact intervened in most industrial policy making, particularly in relation to the automotive industries. As a consequence, policy-making and ideas come from the executive branch and reduce the role of bureaucrats.

As a consequence of the bureaucratic reforms, the state's institutions have linked to politically favoured industrial groups like Proton and Perodua. As Evans (1995b) argues, state bureaucracy requires a certain degree of freedom to be 'connected' with productive groups in the society for economic transformation. Here, connection is the 'embedded linkage' between government and private enterprise to negotiate policy terms to achieve industrial development trajectory. If it is politically captured though, it will compromise the bureaucracy's autonomy to implement coherent industrial policy. In the case of Malaysia, it is unlikely for bureaucrats to act independently due to the executive dominance in the bureaucracy. Freedom to link with other productive groups in the society is constrained by political actors going along with racial considerations. Executive dominance has serious implications on industrial policy implementation. Administrative reforms give rise to politico-bureaucratic ties where the political elite has 'authoritative order' over the bureaucracy. Strong ties between politicians and top officials have become the 'institutional legacy'. Therefore the state bureaucracy's overriding goal is to serve the political master's interest.

The politico-bureaucratic ties have given the political elite capacity to impose its will onto the bureaucracy. Interviews with top officials suggest that they need to work along with the politician's ideas and interests. There is broad influence of political interference making their 'hands tight', especially in the configuration of the national automotive policy. The bureaucracy has limited freedom to formulate automotive policy. Although state agencies like EPU, MITI and MAI conduct studies to improve the NAP, to change aspects of the policy is difficult. Adjusting policy terms is subject to political interference and the need to consider the national car companies and local vendors' interests.

The existing Institutional arrangements have allowed politicians to direct the bureaucracy in interpreting policy to secure the interests of the domestic enterprise. Majority of the respondents have used the term 'policy tweaking' to describe the configuration of the national automotive policy. Policy tweaking is akin to '*layering*' and '*conversion*'. Even though the NAP aims to liberalise the industry, institutional arrangements between the political elite and bureaucracy enable them to 'tweak the policy' in favour of the national car company and vendors linked to its production chains. Special arrangements have taken place between local companies, state officials and politicians to discuss policy tweaking to protect the domestic automotive industry, even though this may go against the interest of top civil servants. According to high ranking official at the Ministry of International Trade and Industry,

> *we have no choice but we need to figure out how to tweak policy to protect the national car company...the national car company is the so-called national interest because there are many vendors linked to the car company's ecosystem.*

Dense ties between politicians and state bureaucracy have shaped policy layering in the NAP, which is not in consonance with the pro-market reforms. This is inevitable because to protect 'local auto carmakers and its vendors that heavily relied on Proton and Perodua to sustain their businesses. In this sense, despite there being pro-market reforms in the domestic automotive industry, the actual practice in the marketplace remains regulated by the government. Though Malaysia is committed to reducing tariffs under the WTO and AFTA obligations, the government introduced excise duties to protect the domestic automotive industry. Malaysia's excise duty imposed on cars is one of the highest in the Southeast Asia region, ranging from 75 per cent to 105 per cent depending on engine capacity. This obviously leads to price discrimination to protect national carmakers.

Although government committed to the obligation of reducing tariffs, however excise duty is the right of the country to impose goods and services. Policy makers can impose higher excise duty for foreign cars. The reason for this is that excise duty is used to offset the significant reduction of tariff barriers which the government has to commit to for progressive liberalisation. The policy tweak gives price advantage to the local auto carmakers that can constitute a direct challenge to the homemade car.

Another example of policy layering in NAP is the localisation policy. Under the TRIMs, localisation policy is considered one of the policies that limits a free business environment in a host economy, as a regulated business environment with the host government imposing measures to favour local firms defeats the principle of national treatment and free business (UNCTAD, 2006; Hoekman, 2005). Since local the content policy is restricted among WTO member governments, the Malaysian government has abolished the localisation policy since 2002. Though has been abolished, the government still can tweak local content policy. One way is to encourage car assemblers to source local components and kits is through excise duty reductions.

Though the government may impose high excise duty for foreign cars but companies will get a tax reduction if the company procure the auto parts and kits from local vendors. This is way for the government to help the local vendor and provide discount for the foreign car company. Respondent suggest that this may be 'policy tweaking' to protect the local vendors. It is also a government strategy for coming up with new rules but with same intention: that is, to encourage more inflow for CKDs. It can promote further linkages with local vendors for technological upscaling and improving productions.

This strategy does not really violate the WTO obligation under TRIMs (Segawa et al., 2014). Furthermore, the TRIMs agreement remains vague in interpretation (Tham, 2014), especially as the agreement continues allowing host governments to impose measures for foreign firms in the areas of human capital development and technological transfers. This creates policy space for most developing countries to interpret sourcing local auto parts and components to assist local firms in developing new products and skills upscaling.

While sourcing local parts and components can reduce excise duties, the actual intention is to enable the national car producers to obtain further excise duty reductions. Every car sold within Malaysia's borders is taxed the same, regardless of make, model, or origin. This is one of the AFTA rules that prevents member nations from discriminating against other foreign companies. However, Proton and Perodua's parts and components are supplied by local vendors since the excise duty rebates are based on the amount of local contents, so with the 90 per cent local content makes the national car producers pay little excise duty. By linking the excise duty reduction scheme with the level of local contents, the national car producers receive a cost advantage in the automotive market. Although the overall market share of the local carmakers has shrunk over the years following 2006's liberalisation, they remain dominant in the domestic automotive market due to less excise duty imposed on both national carmakers.

Interview with top public officers suggest that Linking the local content requirement with excise duty is done to increase economies of scale for the national car company. They suggest that the national car should increase their market share in the local market. According to the head of Malaysia Automotive Institute,

> *…we have a duty to facilitate our homegrown car and obligations to help the local vendors so that they can achieve economies of scale…this is also a national mission to help the Bumiputra vendors in another way….*

The NAP is to facilitate the growth of the domestic automotive industry, including the Industrial Adjustment Fund, Automotive Industrial Fund, and Industrial Linkages Fund. These are offered by the government to support the industry, especially vendors linked to the supply chain for national car producers. Most respondents reveal that the policy tweaking is also an arrangement between the government and politicians to come out with de facto protective measures after liberalisation. The national car project ought to have indirect incentives because as national car producers, the mission is not just purely economic growth but also to encourage the growth of Bumiputra vendors.

The politico-bureaucratic ties enable politicians to direct bureaucrats to implement policy that favours the interest of domestic enterprise. The interview data confirms that most aspects of the NAP are designed to facilitate the national car company to have a greater market share, as one of the top officials at ministry states that, '*as a policy maker imagine the national car is your child, you don't want them to do die if they need help.*'

Politico-bureaucratic ties also facilitate special preferential access to state funds. The government has channelled a substantial amount of funds for Proton to assist in the areas of R&D. According to Mahathir, '*there is a cost for everything we do and we have to deal with it*'. This is due to the fact that the national car company is unable to achieve greater economies of scale, which limits R&D activities. The government needs to provide a fund for R&D activities to increase productivity. The politico-bureaucratic ties have made it easier to mobilise substantial funds to support the growth of the national company. The findings also reveal that special arrangements have been made between the state oil company, Petronas, and Proton, to provide RM30 million to the car company though the board of Petronas does not agree to such funding.

In a developmental state, the key to improving industrial policy is constant negotiation between the bureaucracy and business groups. The government pilot agency is insulated and has less political intervention, which enables the agency to devise more effective industrial upgrading plans with specific groups. However, in the context of Malaysia, politico-bureaucratic ties limit the capacity of the bureaucracy to negotiate with other business groups. Most respondents suggest that strategic planning or changes in the NAP require permission from the 'advisor of Proton'. The bureaucrats have limited say when it comes to the national car project, particularly in searching for strategic partnerships and R&D. Most respondents agreed that they have to work along with the interests of the political elite. Political interference gives the senior officials limited freedom to configure strategy to improve automotive policy planning.

5.4 Conclusion

The above analysis presents the political economy and politics of Malaysia's national automotive policy. The role of institutions, along with a developmentalist state approach, accentuates the strategic role of the state elites (politicians, bureaucrats) and industrial groups (linked to state elites) in configuring national automotive policy. Institutional arrangements taking place by this tripartite arrangement have implications on policy planning and implementation. Despite the fact that the overarching policy intended to liberalise the domestic automotive industry, the dynamic of the politics behind institutional arrangements for the NAP limits pro-market reforms due to vested interest to protect the industry.

Given the longevity of the ruling coalition (UMNO-led BN), political institutions have the capacity to direct the automotive policy in Malaysia's policy-making institutions. Ideas and interest surrounding the NAP are largely manufactured by the political elite. The historical specificity that structures the power relations centred on the executive branch enables the Prime Minister to come out with a specific interest in industrial policy. The idea for the national car project is evidence that the Prime Minister has asserted his interest as part of the heavy industrialisation programme. The existing institutional capacity enables the Prime Minister to pursue his interest as part of industrial development due to the uneven power relations of other political actors. The institutional design structures the power concentration on political elites in UMNO (who dominate the political institutions). The executive branch can therefore can fend off other demands coming from other economic actors, as Campbell (1997a) argues that limited interaction in political institutions due to uneven power relations hinders policy changes.

The national car project under the heavy industrialisation programme shows that the country adopted a developmentalist state approach, where it envisioned transforming the industrial structures to a capital-intensive based economy. While the country holds this economic objective, it is also embedded with the political consideration of Bumiputra interest. Navigating the racial policy and economic development have been central to UMNO's political legitimacy. Bumiputra interest has been infused into the policy-making institutions since the NEP was introduced. Since institutions structure policy options, ethnic consideration has been institutionalised in configuring policy, and it influences the cognitive dimension of political elites in 'packaging' industrial policy. The national car project is interpreted as industrial nationalism with strong emphasis on the development of Bumiputra groups to lead the country's industrial development. It is part of the redistributive programme for the indigenous groups as designated under the NEP. The 'interpretative frame' of the national car project, coloured with racial undertones, became acceptable policy discourse for the ruling elite to support the local car company despite it being uncompetitive.

As a developmental state, the role of institutions in Malaysia facilitates a reciprocal relationship between the government and industrial groups. Like the Northeast Asian developmental state, the government is linked to existing productive groups in the society. However, in the case of Malaysia where there is an absence of industrial groups, the political elite forms such groups to pursue industrial development. Such industrial groups are highly dependent on state resources, even after being privatised, particularly Proton. The collaboration between the government and industrial groups to facilitate heavy industrial development has strengthened patron-client ties over time. The inability of the national car project to arrive at a higher technological frontier while operating on an uneconomical scale accentuates informal linkages to obtain government support. For such reasons, informal rules also become powerful interactions in policy-making institutions among actors to obtain preferential access to state rents. The highly criticised AP system designed for Bumiputra entrepreneurs is also evidence of the patron-client network in action. Despite the fact that the system distorts the level of playing field in the automotive market, political actors have delayed the removal of the system. Such resistance to change is due to the close-knit ties between the AP holders and politicians. The ethnic imperative is also used as part of the discourse to retain the AP system.

Since informal institutions are widely accepted norms in the policy-making institutions of Malaysia, they become a critical part of maintaining and preventing changes in formal rules. The patron-client ties lead to unusual policy arrangements to protect the interest of domestic automotive enterprises by determining prices for foreign cars through informal arrangements and by being ambiguous in the provision of incentives under the NAP. Such unclear information regarding customised incentives is a way to protect domestic automotive industry.

The role of institutions facilitates the politico-bureaucratic ties. While the bureaucracy needs to be insulated from other private demands by political institutions to implement coherent policy, in Malaysia's institutional context the bureaucracies are insulated by political institutions but policy formation is guided by political interest. The bureaucrats have limited freedom to devise strategy in the NAP. The executive dominance in political institutions has the ability to control the state's agency. This makes the bureaucracy subservient to political masters' interests, and as such the political elite can impose their will in the NAP planning and implementation. Furthermore, the bureaucracy is connected to unproductive groups like Proton. Institutional arrangements are formed to further support the groups and the bureaucracy is unable to replace the support due to political interference. This departs from the conventional developmentalist state approach in Northeast Asia whereby the bureaucrats have sufficient freedom to deliberate with specific industrial groups. For this reason, policy layering becomes inevitable against the backdrop of pro-market reforms. The bureaucrats are obliged to interpret policy in favour of domestic interest, thus limiting changes based on the liberalisation initiative under the NAP.

In short, the politics behind the NAP in Malaysia reveal that the institutional arrangements made by the political elite, bureaucracy and industrial groups have powerful implications on Malaysia's automotive industry. The historical specificity, power relations, and normative dimension of Malaysia's institutional context affects the interactions between the principle actors in policy-making institutions. The triangular arrangement between them can rig the allocation of resources and adjust the terms of policy that potentially undermine the overall welfare of the economy. Despite the country having adopted a developmentalist state approach, due to a different institutional context the country has produced different industrial policy and therefore outcomes different than those in Northeast Asia.

References

Abbott, J. (2003). *Developmentalism and dependency in southeast Asia.* London: Routledge.

Abott, J. (2004). 'Not like the rest': Differential development in Malaysia and Thailand. In L. Low (Ed.), *Developmental state: Relevancy, redundancy or reconfiguration?* New York, NY: Nova Science Publisher.

Abdullah, R., Lall, M. K., & Tatsuo, K. (2008). Supplier development framework in the Malaysian automotive industry: Proton's experience. *International Journal of Economics and Management, 2*(1), 29–58.

Beeson, M. (2000). Mahathir and the markets: Globalisation and the pursuit of economic autonomy in Malaysia. *Pacific Affairs, 73*(3), 335–351.

Brown, G. K., Ali, S. H., & Muda, W. M. W. (2004). *Policy lever in Malayia*. Centre for Research on Inequality, Human Security and Ethnicity (CRISE), University of Oxford, Queen Elizabeth House.

Campbell, J. (1997a). Mechanism of evolutionary change in economic governance: Interaction, interpretation and bricolage. *Evolutionary Economics and Path Dependence, 10*(32).

Campbell, J. (1997b). Mechanism of evolutionary change in economic governance: Interaction, interpretation and bricolage. *Evolutionary Economics and Path Dependence, 10*(32).

Case, W. (2012). Microeconomic reform in Malaysia. In H. Hill, S. Y. Tham, & M. Z. Ragayah (Eds.), *Malaysia development challenges: Graduating from the middle*. New York, NY: Routledge.

Chin, J. (2011). Future of democracy in Malaysia. *Panoroma: Insights into Asian and European Affairs, 2*(10), 81–91.

Chin, J. (2015). The cost of Malay supremacy. *The New York Times*. https://www.nytimes.com/2015/08/28/opinion/the-costs-of-malay-supremacy.html.

Dobbin, F. (2004). The sociological view of the economy. In F. Dobbin (Ed.), *The new economic sociology: A reader* (pp. 1–48). Princeton and Oxford: Princeton University Press.

Evans, M. (1995a). Elitism. In D. Marsh & G. Stoker (Eds.), *Theory and methods in political science* (pp. 228-247). Basingstoke: MacMillan.

Evans, P. (1995b). *Embedded autonomy, states and industrial transformation*. Princeton, NJ: Princeton University Press.

Felker, G. (2015). Malaysia's development strategies. In W. Meredith (Ed.), *Routledge handbook of contemporary Malaysia*. Routledge.

Gomez, E. T. (2016). Resisting the fall: The single dominant party, policies and elections in Malaysia. *Journal of Contemporary Asia*.

Gomez, E. T., & Premdas, R. R. (2016). *Affirmative action, ethnicity and conflict*. Routledge.

Hall, P. A., & Taylor, R. C. R. (1996). Political science and the three new institutionalisms. *Political Studies, 44*(5), 936–957.

Hattam, V. C. (1993.) *Labour vision and state power*. Princeton University Press.

Helmke, G., & Levitsky, S. (2004). Informal institutions and comparative politics: A research agenda. *Perspective on Politics, 2*(4), 725–740.

Hoekman, B. (2005). Operationalizing the concept of policy space in the WTO: Beyond special and differential treatment. *Journal of International Economic Law, 8*(2), 405–424.

Jomo, K. S. (2004). Southeast Asian developmental state in comparative East Asian perspectives. In L. Linda (Ed.), *Developmental state: Relevancy, redundancy or reconfiguration?* Nova Publishers.

Lim, K. S. (2005). *Who is the king of APs? Making public AP holders In the national Interest*. Parliament speech. https://dapmalaysia.org/all-archive/English/2005/jun05/lge/lge131.htm.

Livelifedrive. (2013). *Explaining the mystery behind high car prices in Malaysia—Part 1*. http://www.livelifedrive.com/news/explaining-mystery-behind-high-car-prices-malaysia-part-1/28229.

Lowndes, V. (2010). The institutional approach. In D. Marsh & G. Stoker (Eds.), *Theory and method in political science*. London: Palgrave Macmillan.

Mahoney, J., & Thelen, K. (2010). A theory of gradual institutional change. In M. James & T. Kathleen (Eds.), *Explaining institutional change: Ambiguity, agency, and power*. New York, NY: Cambridge University Press.

Malaysia Customs Act. (1967). *Customs (rules of valuation) regulations 1999*. http://www.customs.gov.my/en/ip/Pages/ip_act.aspx.

Milner, A., Embong, A. R., & Tham, S. Y. (Eds). (2014). *Transforming Malaysia dominant and competing paradigms*. Cambridge University Press.

Ministry of International Trade and Industry Malaysia (MITI). (2014). *Review of national automotive policy: MITI advances the Government of Malaysia's agenda of liberalisation, paving the way for a more competitive automotive industry for domestic, regional and global markets*. http://www.miti.gov.my/index.php/pages/view/1449.

Moon, C. I., & Prasad, R. (1994). Beyond the developmental state: Network, politics and institutions. *Governance: An International Journal of Policy Administration and Institutions, 7*(4), 360–386.

National Automotive Policy (NAP). (2016). http://www.maa.org.my/pdf/NAP_2019_policy.pdf.

News Straits Times. (2016). *Govt approves RM1.5 billion soft loan for Proton to pay vendors*. https://www.nst.com.my/news/2016/04/138054/govt-approves-rm15-billion-soft-loan-proton-pay-vendors.

North, D. (1990). *Institutions, institutional change, and economic performance*. New York: Cambridge University Press.

Paultan. (2014). *Mazda SkyActiv cars prequalified as EEV—reports*. https://paultan.org/2014/01/22/reports-mazda-skyactiv-pre-qualified-eev-incentives/.

Penang Institute. (2017). *The government's heavy hand in setting car prices*. http://penanginstitute.org/v3/media-centre/penang-institute-in-the-news/533-the-government-s-heavy-hand-in-setting-car-prices.

Pierson, P. (1993). When effect becomes cause: Policy feedback and political change. *World Politics, 45*, 595–628.

Segawa, N., Natsuda, K., & Thoburn, J. (2014). Affirmative action and economic liberalisation: the dilemmas of the Malaysian automotive industry. *Asian Studies Review, 38*(3), 422–441.

Tan, J. (2015). Rent seeking and money politics in Malaysia: Ethnicity, cronyism and class. In W. Meredith (Ed.), *Routledge handbook of contemporary Malaysia*. New York, NY: Routledge.

Tham, S. Y. (2014). Trade policy formulation in Malaysia: Navigating between the economic and race paradigms. In A. Milner, A. R. Embong, & S. Y. Tham (Eds.), *Transforming Malaysia dominant and competing paradigms*. Cambridge University Press.

The Star. (2010). *Mokhzani Mahathir passes Porsche rights to Sime*. http://www.thestar.com.my/business/business-news/2010/02/03/mokhzani-mahathir-passes-porsche-rights-to-sime/#PFFZ09sDPY1jEV1W.99.

The Sun Daily. (2016). *APs a 'cash cow' to the holders*. https://www.thesundaily.my/archive/1668820-BSARCH346540.

Thelen, K., & Steinmo, S. (1992). Historical institutionalism in comparative politics. In S. Steinmo, K. Thelen, & F. Longstreth (Eds.), *Structuring politics: Historical institutionalism in comparative analysis* (pp. 1–32). Cambridge: Cambridge University Press.

UNCTAD. (2006). *Trade and development report*, 2006. New York, NY: United Nations Conference on Trade and Development.

World Trade Organisation. (2017). *Agreement on implementation of Article VII of the general agreement on tariffs and trade 1994 (GATTS)*. https://www.wto.org/English/docs_e/legal_e/20-val_01_e.htm.

Chapter 6
Conclusion

6.1 Valuable Insights from This Study

This research aims to explore the political economy of industrial policy-making institutions in Malaysia, particularly in its national automotive policy. This study seeks to explore the institutional arrangements that evolve around the national automotive policy. Given that institutional structures underpin the strategic role of the state elite (politicians and bureaucrats) and 'selected' business groups in policy-making institutions, this study also aims to explore how these economic actors mobilise, coordinate, and prioritise resources and economic preferences in the policy-making institutions. This study reveals the political economy of Malaysia's policy-making institutions, which have not been widely explored particularly the national automotive policy.

The empirical investigation from this research presents that the triangular arrangement between the political elite, bureaucrats and selected enterprises (in this case the national carmaker and its vendors) represents the crucial economic actors in policy formulation and implementations. However, power relations are centred around the Prime Minister's Office. Concentration of power has implications on policy direction. The political agenda and preferences are thus manufactured by the ruling elite. This is inevitable due to the longevity of UMNO-led Barisan Nasional dominating the political institutions. This arrangement has also developed strong politico-bureaucratic ties that enable the ruling elite to impose their will into the bureaucracy. Strong political influences limit the freedom of the bureaucracy, which is at the heart of policy implementation. The main government agencies such as MITI, EPU and MIDA have limited freedom to devise policy. In most policy-making processes the bureaucrats' 'hands are tied', and though they are supposed to play advisory role, the priority of the policy is likely to advance or maintain the interests of the political elite.

The strong politico-bureaucratic ties also worked to maintain the interest of the selected business enterprises who have close connections with the political elite. These selected business groups, including the national carmaker and Bumiputra entrepreneurs who engage in the automotive sectors, are created by the political elite. The creation of the Bumiputra industrial class is meant to enable the group to

F. Suffian, *Political Economy of Malaysia's Industrial Policy*,
https://doi.org/10.1007/978-981-33-6901-6_6

lead the industrial development of the country. Their development in the automotive sectors has been heavily dependent on government resources.

The government has framed the automotive industry as nationalist economic project which includes the localisation policy, AP system and the national car project. Most programmes and policy introduced around automotive sectors are mainly to pursue domestic economic transformation, and more crucially, the development of Bumiputra business groups. In this sense, elite policy actors resist or seek ways to protect any pro-market reforms that undermine the interests of Bumiputra business groups. However, liberalising the automotive industry is inevitable because the government has to maintain a market-friendly environment for foreign and other auto companies in the domestic automotive industry, which is typical in the developmentalist state approach. The institutions of a developmentalist state enable policy actors to design market entry in a way to protect domestic interests. The existing institutional structures in Malaysia support reciprocal relations between state actors (political elites and bureaucrats) and selected business groups. Interaction between these actors enables come out with 'unusual policy arrangements' to protect the interest of the national carmaker and Bumiputra vendors. This involves policy tweaking, which is linked to *layering* and *conversion*[1] as part of 'mobilisation of bias' by policy elites.

The existing institutional structures facilitate a reciprocal relationship between the government and 'selected' industrial groups that is crucial to support the growth of the automotive industry. It has also institutionalised the patron-client network (informal institutions) which has formed a routine or culture that influences the behaviour of economic actors. Furthermore, the racial consideration in economic development has accentuated the patronage system, particularly between Bumiputra groups and the political elite. Informal institutions becomes standard operating procedures that reflect 'how things are done', including policy tweaking among political and Bumiputra business actors.

Given that there is a weak link between the political institutions and societal groups in Malaysia, compounded by uneven power relations in the policy-making institutions, the domestic institutional design enables the political elite to fend off other economic actor interests who oppose the projects. The executive dominance in the policy-making process enables the elite to transfer resources and adjust policy in favour of the growth of the national car projects, despite there being no comparative advantage. The institutional context that structured the power relations centred around the executive branch enables the political elite to suppress other sectional groups' interests. This features the institutional capacity in the developmentalist state approach, where the ruling elite are able to impose their will in the developmental agenda. This can be seen in the considerable amount of funds allocated for physical infrastructures, production plants, technological investments and research and development to support the domestic automotive sector.

[1]Layering is the creation of new rules together with old ones, but change occurs not through the displacement of old rules, rather through the addition of new ones on top of old ones. Conversion is when rules remain formally the same but are interpreted and enacted differently (Mahoney & Thelen, 2010, p. 17).

Empirical assessment shows that the national automotive policy is constrained by the interest of the national car projects, especially Proton. The presence of the national car project has limited pro-market reforms and has made policy inconsistent. Under the rubric of 'national interest', coordination between elite policy actors to ensure that Proton has some advantageous position over non-national cars. It can be argued that the national car project is able to compete in the market based on government reciprocal relationships accentuated by a deeply embedded patron-client network. This is inevitable because the national car project was created by political elite and the growth of Proton has been highly dependent on economic rents since the outset of the heavy industrialisation programme. The dependence on economic rents is part of the policy legacies (associated with path dependence). Once rent-seeking has been institutionalised, it becomes an 'intergenerational' transfer in the policy-making process. Furthermore, the creation of Proton is associated with the development of the Bumiputra industrialist class that is dependent on the government, so it is difficult to be removed in the institutional setting.

The role of institutions in Malaysia has limited the growth of Proton. There is excessive political interference which become institutional constraints, hence compromised the growth of Proton. The national car company has limited freedom in most management decisions. The political elite has strong influence on the direction of the company and its technological upgrading. Though political influence is crucial for the growth of Proton, too much interference have made the national car company less competitive. This makes the company reliant on the domestic automotive market and further accentuates the role of elite policy actors in maintaining the company's interest in the market.

Political factors and nationalism have become institutional constraints for national carmakers forming partnerships. The empirical analysis shows that the national carmaker represents national pride and major development of the Bumiputra industrialist class. Partnership agreements usually may entail ceding management control of the national car company. This has been a challenging task for Proton, because in ceding control the new management is likely to undermine the Bumiputra interest in Proton and its vendors. Recent development saw that Proton join collaboration with Geely Zhe Jiang, this seen as positive move by the government to improve Proton efficiency. Though this partnership intends to reforms Proton, however institutional arrangements can take place to secure Bumiputra interests given the government has to protect the ethno-economic interest.

In summary, the role of institutions in Malaysia has facilitated the growth of the automotive sector, as the existing institutional capacity has enabled the elite to shift resources, adjust policy and coordinate policy actors to develop the domestic automotive industry and form the national car project. Political elite managed to shift the comparative advantage of the state which was previously limited. More crucially, the Bumiputra industrialist class was created through the national car project. The strategic role of the state elite (politicians and bureaucracy) and the national carmaker enabled them to respond to trade liberalisation (through institutional arrangements) that could potentially affect their interest in automotive sectors. The tripartite arrangements enable the national carmaker to sustain in the market competitions while preserving the Bumiputra interest. Though the role of institutions facilitates the growth of the domestic automotive industry, it has also constrained the growth of the industry and the national car company. Elite policy makers are unable to be flexible in policy changes in the NAP due to vested interest. Opening the automotive market can improve efficiency but competing on a level playing field can undermine the national car company and the Bumiputra industrialist class interest. The patronage system and political interference has led to rigidity in the NAP. A strong political grip in configuring the NAP has compromised coherent policy implementation.

6.2 Concluding Remarks

This study shows the political economy of policy-making institutions in Malaysia. The empirical analysis presented shows institutional arrangements made by actors and how the dynamics of political economy can influence the policy-making process in the automotive industry in Malaysia's institutional setting. Institutions matter, but the institutional context influenced by history, power relations, political factors and embedded conventions is also crucial to understand the complex relationships and interactions among policy actors. This has implications in policy-making institutions, which in turn affects their developmental strategy as discussed in this research.

The major concern of industrial development in Malaysia does not lie in the policy, but rather in the country-specific institutions and excessive response to domestic political economy demand. To balance between the industrial accumulation and nationalist interest is difficult, however there is a need to relax the ethno-nationalist stance, reduce rent-seekers' interest (especially the unproductive groups) and reassess industrial development with economic rationale. The growth of Thailand, Indonesia and China in the automotive production network will continue to pressure Malaysia's automotive sectors. Protecting 'national interest' at the expense of public funds for almost four decades, there is a need to re-examine the interest of 'a national champion' with market discipline. Less emphasis on ethno-nationalism is critical for the automotive sector to grow. It is not worth maintaining 'national interest' if it is unable to be competitive.

Given the existing policy-making institutions, the future challenge for Malaysia's industrial development will be to graduate into a higher technological frontier. This will be difficult, as Malaysia's industrialisation progress can be 'stuck in the middle', or what Henderson and Phillips (2006) echoed as the 'stalling of Malaysia's industrialisation project'. This means that the country will (or has begun to) shift focus to service sectors (for example finance) as a new source of growth. Focusing on the service sector can eventually accelerate 'a premature deindustrialisation process', where the country has failed to progress in manufacturing sectors (or falls in value-added manufacturing productivity). While focusing on service sectors is important to generate country revenue, it should not be the handmaiden of capital accumulation. The investment in value-added manufacturing remains crucial to make progressive and sustainable economic growth. Industrial development is the source of technological advancement. Malaysia has invested substantially in industrial development and the country has the necessary resources to grow, provided that it maintains focus and improve its institutions.

There is a need to further research the role of the institutions and the growth of the national car project, particularly the technological upgrading. While this research was conducted, new development has also occurred in Proton. The long overdue search for partnership for Proton now has been sealed with Geely Zhejiang, which also owns Volvo. It would be interesting to research the technological transfer between the Chinese company and Proton. This is crucial for Proton to upgrade existing technology in order to improve economies of scale and access a wider export market. Changes in the NAP are expected as well after this partnership agreement, which would be interesting to assess, including changes in future policy terms and in the role of institutions in this area.

References

Henderson, J., & Phillips, R. (2006). Unintended consequences: Social policy, state institutions and the 'stalling' of the Malaysian industrialization project. *Economy and Society, 36*(1).

Mahoney, J., & Thelen. K. (2010). A theory of gradual institutional change. In M. James & T. Kathleen (Eds.), *Explaining institutional change: Ambiguity, agency, and power*. New York: Cambridge University Press.

Index

F. Suffian, *Political Economy of Malaysia's Industrial Policy*,
https://doi.org/10.1007/978-981-33-6901-6

www.ingramcontent.com/pod-product-compliance
Ingram Content Group UK Ltd.
Pitfield, Milton Keynes, MK11 3LW, UK
UKHW021957040925
462611UK00004B/444
* 9 7 8 9 8 1 3 3 6 9 0 0 9 *